# Community Builders

## 50 Exercises for Church Groups

**Rochelle Melander**
**Harold Eppley**

SMALL GROUP SERIES

Augsburg Fortress, Minneapolis

**INTERSECTIONS**
Small Group Series

**Community Builders**
50 Exercises for Church Groups

Developed in cooperation with the Division for Congregational Ministries, Evangelical Lutheran Church in America

Rochelle Melander and Harold Eppley, writers
Andrea Lee Schieber, Ron Klug, Ann Terman Olson, James Satter, editors
The Wells Group, series design
Cover photo © PhotoDisc, Inc.

**Acknowledgments**
The writers wish to thank the people of Nativity Lutheran Church in Wauwatosa, Wisconsin, Advent Lutheran Church in Cedarburg, Wisconsin, and Cross of Life Lutheran Church in Brookfield, Wisconsin.

Scripture quotations are from New Revised Standard Version Bible, copyright 1989 Division of Christian Education of the National Council of the Churches of Christ in the United States of America. Used by permission.

Manufactured in U.S.A.
1 2 3 4 5 6 7 8 9 0 1 2 3 4 5 6 7 8 9

# Contents

# Contents

# Introduction

## A new vision of small group ministry

Our Savior's Church boasts a thriving small group ministry program. A few years into their program, many of the participants talked enthusiastically about how small groups had changed their lives. They expressed a desire to share the blessings of this ministry with church members outside of the small group program.

Two of Our Savior's church leaders suggested incorporating small group ministry components into church committee meetings. Marta, a member of the parenting small group and the church council, encouraged the council to end each meeting by sharing prayer concerns and praying for one another. Steve, a discipleship group participant and member of the youth task force, suggested that the task force begin its meetings with a brief biblical reflection time. Slowly and intentionally, small group members began to use the small group ministry process to breathe life into the committees of Our Savior's Church.

Today at Our Savior's, every church group uses these components from the small group program to begin and end their meetings: prayer, mutual support, and biblical reflection. As a result, Our Savior's members feel more connected to each other and to the ministry they do together. Committee members who had never tried small groups have liked what they experienced and some have joined small groups. As a result, the church's small group ministry program has grown. But most important, the members of Our Savior's who serve on committees and task forces are now spiritually fed as they meet to do their work.

## What is a small group?

Roberta Hestenes, a Presbyterian pastor and author, defines a small group as an intentional face-to-face gathering of three to twelve people who meet regularly with the common purpose of discovering and growing in the possibilities of the abundant life in Christ.

Many churches offer three types of small groups. In *discipleship groups* people gather to grow in the Christian faith and life. *Support and recovery groups* focus on special interests, concerns, or needs—such as coping with grief. *Ministry groups* have a task-oriented focus and include church councils and other committees.

## Small groups in history

For centuries small groups have helped people connect with God and one another. Moses, with the help of his father-in-law Jethro, created small groups to handle disputes within their wilderness community. Jesus taught and told stories in small groups. In the early church, Christians assembled weekly in one another's homes for prayer, mutual support, and Scripture study (see Acts 2:44-47).

Christians have used small groups to ignite commitment within the church. Men's and women's monasteries, such as those founded in the fourth century by Pachomius and his sister Mary, provided an opportunity for Christians to gather daily in small groups for worship. Beginning in 1739, John Wesley initiated Methodist classes of twelve members that met weekly in homes for prayer and biblical study. In the twentieth century, Dorothy Day organized the Catholic Workers Movement, providing a structure for small groups of Christians to participate in worship and acts of mercy.

## Who can use this book?

This book is a resource for ministry groups that seek to integrate small group components of prayer, mutual support, and biblical reflection into their meetings. The book provides a process that will both build community and strengthen the work the group does together.

*Community Builders* can be used by groups that meet regularly to do the work of the congregation: for example, church councils, committees, and task forces, altar guilds, and musical groups. It can also be used by groups that meet infrequently or for specific work projects.

The exercises in this book are presented in an easy-to-use format, requiring little advance preparation. Any member of the group can facilitate these exercises. Some groups invite members to take turns. The exercise leader or facilitator needs no special training. Teaching, learning, and spiritual growth result from the group experience of praying, sharing, reflecting on the Scriptures, and working together. The facilitator is the person designated to set the pace, keep the group focused, and enable group members to support and care for one another.

## How to use this book

### Discussing the process

If you plan to use this book regularly with your ministry group, begin by providing some information about the process.

Each Community Builder, thematically centered, has four primary components: an opening prayer, gathering time, biblical reflection, and a closing prayer.

Community building works best when all group members understand the purpose and benefits of these exercises. Explaining the purpose behind the process is especially important for existing groups that are comfortable with their current meeting style and content. Ministry group members are often task-oriented and may see the community building process as intrusive. In addition, ministry groups meet less frequently than most small groups, so it may take more time to build community than it would in support and recovery groups, for example, which meet more frequently.

Invite the members of your group to think of community building time as offering their first fruits to God. The Bible encourages Christians to give to God the first of what they earn and possess: money, time, and talents. Giving to God the first minutes of your meeting time together can serve as a powerful reminder that all the time you have is a gift from God and all the work you do is blessed by God.

### Deciding on an agenda

These exercises are designed to take between fifteen and twenty-five minutes to complete. Discuss with the group both the amount of time they want to allot for these exercises and how they want to incorporate the exercises into their meeting.

The agendas below suggest two possible ways of using these exercises. If time is limited, you may choose not to answer all of the biblical reflection questions.

---

**Agenda** (*60-minute meeting*)
Opening prayer: 1 minute
Gathering time: 5-10 minutes
Biblical reflection: 5-10 minutes
Business/task: 35-45 minutes
Closing prayer: 4 minutes

**Agenda** (*90-minute meeting*)
Opening prayer: 1 minute
Gathering time: 5-10 minutes
Business/task: 65-75 minutes
Biblical reflection: 5-10 minutes
Closing prayer: 4 minutes

## Choosing Community Builders

The Community Builders are grouped thematically (see Contents, pages 3-4). The title of each section and each Community Builder indicates its theme. The exercises are arranged according to the various aspects of a ministry group's life. Some of the exercises focus on specific issues a ministry group might encounter, such as setting goals. Other exercises center on more general spiritual themes, like receiving God's blessings as you work. Select exercises from the list as your needs dictate. Some exercises may not apply to your group.

## Facilitating the exercises

*Prayer* The prayers take various formats, inviting different levels of participation from group members. Tell group members that at times they will be asked, if they are willing, to pray aloud. Learning to pray aloud takes time and practice. If group members feel uncomfortable, invite them to start with the shortest prayers.

The opening prayers introduce the theme for the Community Builder. As the facilitator, you may lead the opening prayer or ask a group member to do so.

The closing prayers end the group meeting. Always provide an opportunity during the closing prayers for group members to share their own prayer requests. Your group can benefit from taking a moment to honor these requests and pray for one another. (See the closing prayers in Community Builders 24, 26, and 35 for information about how to integrate prayer requests into a closing prayer.) Encourage group members to pray for each other between meetings.

*Gathering questions* Group members are encouraged to respond to one of three personal gathering questions. These offer an opportunity for group members to share experiences from their lives. It is important that you take time to answer these questions. If you skip this section, the community building process will be less effective. The gathering questions function to create an atmosphere of trust and openness and enable group members to get to know one another better. Through answering these questions, group members gain confidence to answer the biblical questions. The gathering questions also focus the group around the theme and lead into the biblical reflection time.

As the facilitator, introduce all the questions in this section either by reading them aloud or posting them on newsprint or a chalkboard. In some circumstances, especially with groups that know each other well, you may want to choose one gathering question for all group members to answer. Tell group members that they will each be given an opportunity to respond. Allow group members to modify the questions or to pass.

At your first meeting, or when new people are present, have the group members introduce themselves during Gathering Time. Then, briefly present your answer to one of the questions. Go around the group, allowing everyone an opportunity to respond.

*Biblical reflection* This component includes a paragraph about the Bible text, a biblical passage, and questions relating the text to the life and work of your group. The biblical reflection time is not centered on learning biblical content but on building relationships with God and one another.

Read the statement about the text to the group. Then, have someone read the text, either from the book or the Bible. Ask the questions in order, allowing time for responses. You do not need to get responses from everyone for every question.

## Some final reminders

It may be helpful to form a group covenant—a shared agreement that states the group's purpose, mission, and the responsibilities of the group members. (For more information about writing a group covenant see *Starting Small Groups and Keeping Them Going*, pages 53-54.) A group covenant can address some of the issues below.

- Group members are never required to answer questions, read aloud, or pray.

- The exercises are not designed to encourage the sharing of "deep dark secrets." Even so, confidentiality is important and group members need to keep confidential the stories and prayer concerns shared in the meeting.

- Group members need to agree together to participate in non-judgmental behavior. Group members may confess their own shortcomings, if appropriate, not those of others. Group members should not give advice unless asked for it.

- Group members are encouraged to be accountable to one another— responsible to each other and open to change.

It might be helpful to ask group members to commit to doing these exercises for an entire year. This will help prevent group members from dropping the exercises after only one or two times.

## Give it time

Community building time may sound like a radical idea to some church members. If this is a new concept for your congregation, it will probably take awhile for people to grow comfortable with the process. Be patient, pray, and give it time.

# Resource list

## Foundational

*Starting Small Groups—and Keeping Them Going.* Minneapolis: Augsburg Fortress, 1995. This comprehensive guide provides information on the biblical foundation for small group ministry, a step-by-step plan for creating a small group ministry program, training materials for educating facilitators, and reproducible worksheets for training facilitators.

*Turning Committees into Communities,* by Roberta Hestenes. Colorado Springs: Navpress, 1991. This 32-page book provides basic helps to guide committees as they seek to become caring, Christian communities.

## Small group guides

*Intersections Small Group Series.* Minneapolis: Augsburg Fortress, 1995. The series includes the following study guides for discipleship and support and recovery groups.

*The Bible and Life: God's Message for Today,* by Joy P. Clarke. Explores the basic message of the Bible and how it serves as a means of divine grace.

*Captive and Free: Insights from Galatians,* by Walter F. Taylor Jr. A study of Galatians that addresses God's gift of freedom from destructive patterns to a liberating freedom.

*Caring and Community: Perspectives from Ephesians,* by Robert H. Albers. This study focuses on the important life support we gain through Christian fellowship in an age of personal isolation.

*Death and Grief: Healing through Group Support,* by Harold Ivan Smith. Helps those who grieve to bring their stories, anger, and bewilderment to a small group.

*Divorce: Survival and Hope,* by Russell E. Fink and Barbara Owen-Fink. Guides divorced and separated people in dealing with the transition from being married to being single.

*Faith: Confidence and Doubt in Daily Life*, by Martin E. Marty. A study that helps groups explore personal faith in life-cycle experiences— moods and situations, joy and discouragement, confidence and doubt.

*Following Jesus: Encouragement from the Beatitudes for a Troubled World*, by George S. Johnson. Helps participants move beyond a world dominated by greed, violence, and domination to one of compassion, harmony, and community.

*Jesus: Divine and Human*, by John L. Heagle. Explores what a difference it can make to have Jesus as a Savior, teacher, healer, reconciler, and friend.

*Men and Women: Building Communication*, by Tina and Dennis Korte. Examines male-female relationships, differences, and commonalities and helps develop skills to improve communication between men and women.

*Peace: Christian Living in a Violent World*, by Mary I. Farr. A Bible study that explores the peace of God and what wholeness and health, contentment, and security mean for one's life.

*Praying: Meeting God in Daily Life*, by Lyn Klug. A Bible study that examines the depth and power of prayer, the personal nature and lifestyle of prayer, and a variety of prayer forms and occasions.

*Self-Esteem: Encouraging Self and Others*, by Eddie Jane Pelkey and Irene Getz. Participants explore the sometimes-difficult balance between loving self and acting responsibly toward others.

*Smart Choices: Making Your Way through Life*, by Rochelle Melander and Harold Eppley. Helps group members explore and follow principles for living that are consistent with Christianity.

## Additional small group resources

*Fun Friend-making Activities for Adult Groups*, by Karen Dockrey. Loveland, Colo.: Group Publishing Incorporated, 1997.

*LifeStories: The Christian Version*, created by Wilfred Bockelman, Truman Howell, and Vivian Johnson. Pomona, Calif.: Talicore, 1994. Available by calling Talicore at 1-800-433-GAME. A board game that helps people share their stories and enjoy conversation.

*Rituals and Icebreakers: Practical Tools for Forming Community*, by Kathleen O. Chesto. Kansas City, Mo.: Sheed and Ward, 1995.

*Sharing Your Faith with Friends, Relatives, and Neighbors*, by Paul Sorensen. Minneapolis: Augsburg Fortress, 1995. A six session small group process for building faith-sharing skills. Participant book and leader guide available.

## Community Builder 1

# Getting Acquainted

## Opening prayer

**Instruct the group that each time the leader says, "We have gathered in your name," the group will respond, "Be present among us."**

Leader:     Jesus, leader and friend, enrich our life together. We have gathered in your name,

Group:      Be present among us.

Leader:     Guide us as we work together. We have gathered in your name,

Group:      Be present among us.

Leader:     Bless the work we do for you. We have gathered in your name,

Group:      Be present among us.

## Gathering time

**Ask each person in the group to say his or her name and then respond to one of the following:**

■ Tell about what you love to do in your spare time.

■ Describe what you do on a typical day.

■ Tell something about yourself that no one else in the group knows.

## Biblical reflection

**Read this paragraph to the group:**

Throughout the Gospel of Matthew, Jesus emphasizes the importance of Christian community. Matthew is the only one of the four Gospels that uses the term "church" (for example, Matthew 16:18 and 18:17). In this passage, Jesus assures his followers that he will be present whenever they worship and serve in his name.

**Have someone read this passage aloud:**

Matthew 18:20:
[Jesus said] **20**"For where two or three are gathered in my name, I am there among them."

**Invite group members to respond to the questions printed below. If time is limited, choose the questions that best meet your group's needs:**

1. Describe a time when you experienced Christ's presence while gathered with other people.

2. What are your expectations about being in this group?

3. What about the work of this group do you hope to find fulfilling?

4. What questions do you have about participating in this group?

## Closing prayer

**Pray this prayer aloud:**

*Welcoming God, we thank you for the people you have brought together to be a part of this group: (insert group members' names). Help us to grow spiritually as we minister together in your name. Amen*

## Community Builder 2 | Growing Together Spiritually

## Opening prayer

**Pray the following prayer aloud:**

Emmanuel, God with us, we rejoice in the opportunity to grow closer to you and to one another. Dwell with us as we meet, unite us as we work, and awaken us to your presence. Amen

## Gathering time

**Ask each person in the group to respond to one of the following:**

■ Tell why you joined this congregation.

■ Share what you most enjoy about being part of this church.

■ Tell about one of your favorite church memories.

## Biblical reflection

**Read this paragraph to the group:**

Paul wrote to the Christians in the city of Colossae from prison. He advised them about how to combat teachers of false doctrine. In these verses, Paul encourages the Christians in Colossae to attend to the spiritual aspects of their lives.

**Have someone read this passage aloud:**

Colossians 3:16-17:
**16**Let the word of Christ dwell in you richly; teach and admonish one another in all wisdom; and with gratitude in your hearts sing psalms, hymns, and spiritual songs to God. **17**And whatever you do, in word or deed, do everything in the name of the Lord Jesus, giving thanks to God the Father through him.

**Invite group members to respond to the questions printed below. If time is limited, choose the questions that best meet your group's needs:**

1. Read what Paul says in verse 17 again. What do these words mean in terms of our work as a group?

2. What does it mean to grow spiritually?

3. In what ways have you been spiritually nurtured by the Christian community?

4. What can we do, both in and outside of group meetings, to help each other grow spiritually?

## Closing prayer

**Tell the group that you will be giving them two to three minutes for silent prayer. Ask them to use that time to pray for one another, the group, and its spiritual growth.**

## Community Builder 3 — Making a Commitment to the Group

## Opening prayer

**Instruct the group that each time the leader says, "Teach us to live our lives," the group will respond, "Rooted and built up in you."**

Leader: Christ, you are the vine and we are the branches. Give us the courage to commit to our tasks and teach us to live our lives,

Group: Rooted and built up in you.

Leader: Nurture us with your love and plant in us the desire to support one another in our duties. Teach us to live our lives,

Group: Rooted and built up in you.

## Gathering time

**Ask each person in the group to respond to one of the following:**

■ Tell about a group you once belonged to and explain why it was important to you. For example, you might talk about a school band, a sports team, or a community group.

■ Describe a project that took you a long time to complete.

■ Tell about a faithful friend or pet.

## Biblical reflection

**Read this paragraph to the group:**

Some of the members of the church at Colossae had come to believe in and worship angels and other spirits. Their new doctrine, considered by Paul to be faulty, mixed beliefs borrowed from various religious traditions. In this passage, Paul reminds the Colossians to live their lives rooted in Christ.

**Have someone read this passage aloud:**

Colossians 2:6-7:
[6]As you therefore have received Christ Jesus the Lord, continue to live your lives in him, [7]rooted and built up in him and established in the faith, just as you were taught, abounding in thanksgiving.

**Invite group members to respond to the questions printed below. If time is limited, choose the questions that best meet your group's needs:**

1. What do you think it means to be "rooted and built up in [Christ] and established in the faith" (Colossians 2:7)?

2. When you have been part of a group in the past, what has helped you to remain faithful to that group?

3. What can each of us do to make a commitment to this group and its tasks?

4. What can we do to help each other honor that commitment?

## Closing prayer

**Begin by praying the following prayer aloud:**

*Jesus, source of our strength, we pray for everyone gathered here, that we might be strengthened by you in our commitment to this group and our work together.*

**Ask group members to name the person on their right, saying:**

*We pray for (name).*

**Continue until all have been named.**

## Community Builder 4

# Building Trust Together

## Opening prayer

**Pray the following prayer aloud:**

God, our rock and salvation, you are the one on whom we depend. Teach us to be trustworthy. Free us from our fears so that we can trust one another. Amen

## Gathering time

**Ask each person in the group to respond to one of the following:**

■ Describe a time when you needed to rely on the skill or expertise of another.

■ Share an experience of being trusted by another person.

■ Tell about one of your valuables that would be difficult for you to entrust to another person.

## Biblical reflection

**Read this paragraph to the group:**

God led Moses and the people of Israel out of slavery in Egypt and into the wilderness, enroute to the promised land. Since being freed, Moses had spent each day judging the many disputes of the Israelites. In this text Jethro, Moses' father-in-law, encourages Moses to appoint people to serve as leaders over small groups of Israelites and help settle disputes.

**Have someone read this passage aloud:**

Exodus 18:21-22:
[Jethro said], **21**"You should also look for able men among all the people, men who fear God, are trustworthy, and hate dishonest gain; set such men over them as officers over thousands, hundreds, fifties and tens. **22** Let them sit as judges for the people at all times; let them bring every important case to you, but decide every minor case themselves. So it will be easier for you, and they will bear the burden with you."

**Invite group members to respond to the questions printed below. If time is limited, choose the questions that best meet your group's needs:**

1. According to the text and your own experience, what does it mean to be trustworthy?

2. What prevents people from trusting one another?

3. Share examples of how you have seen group members who trust each other work together effectively.

4. What can we do to help build trust in our group?

# Closing prayer

**Ask group members to create the closing prayer by completing the following sentence as it pertains to the group's work:**

*Trustworthy God, help us to _____ one another (for example, love).*

**Write the group's answers on chalkboard or newsprint. As your closing prayer, have the group read the sentence aloud using each of the verbs you have listed. For example:**

*Help us to love one another; help us to serve one another.*

**As the leader, conclude by praying aloud:**

*Trustworthy God, in all that we do, build trust among us. Amen*

## Community Builder 5

# Recalling How God Has Blessed Us in the Past

## Opening prayer

**Pray the following prayer aloud:**

Holy God of wonders, just as you led the people of Israel through the sea, you have guided us to this day. We thank you for blessing our past. Open our eyes and ears so that we may see and hear the wonders that surround us. Amen

## Gathering time

**Ask each person in the group to respond to one of the following:**

- Tell about a time when someone surprised you by doing a good deed for you.

- Tell about an experience with water.

- Describe a wonder that you have witnessed.

## Biblical reflection

**Read this paragraph to the group:**

In times of both difficulty and joy, the people of Israel remembered how God had saved them in the past. The writer of this passage reminds the listeners of how God had delivered the people of Israel from the Egyptians by allowing them to pass through the Red Sea.

**Have someone read this passage aloud:**

Psalm 77:11, 15, 19-20:
[11]I will call to mind the deeds of the LORD; I will remember your wonders of old. . . . [15] With your strong arm you redeemed your people, the descendants of Jacob and Joseph. . . . [19] Your way was through the sea, your path, through the mighty waters; yet your footprints were unseen. [20]You led your people like a flock by the hand of Moses and Aaron.

**Invite group members to respond to the questions printed below. If time is limited, choose the questions that best meet your group's needs:**

1. Why do you think it was important for the people of Israel to remember how God had helped them in the past?

2. What significant events in our congregation's or group's history are important for us to remember?

3. In verse 19 the psalmist wrote that "[God's] footprints were unseen." What does this say about the nature of God's guidance?

4. Describe a time when you felt that God was leading our group, even though God's footprints were unseen.

5. In what ways is God currently leading our group and working wonders among us?

## Closing prayer

**Tell group members that you will be offering a prayer in which they will be invited to name some of the wonders for which they are thankful. Then pray:**

*Wonderful God, we thank you for the wonders that we name both aloud and silently in our hearts. . . .*

## Community Builder 6

# Discovering Our Gifts

## Opening prayer

**Pray the following prayer aloud:**

God, giver of all good gifts, you have made us who we are. Assist us in discovering what you have already given to us—our abilities and our talents—so that we may use them to glorify you. Amen

## Gathering time

**Ask each person in the group to respond to one of the following:**

■ Tell about an ability you have always wanted to have and don't. Why is it important to you?

■ Describe one of the favorite gifts you have received. What made this gift so special?

■ What are the most helpful words someone has spoken to you and why?

## Biblical reflection

**Read this paragraph to the group:**

The First Letter of Peter was written to Christians experiencing persecution for their faith. Some scholars believe that these Christians were also experiencing conflict within their community. The section in which this passage appears instructs Christians about their life together, reminding them that each of them has been uniquely gifted by God to serve the common good.

1 Peter 4:10-11:
**10** Like good stewards of the manifold grace of God, serve one another with whatever gift each of you has received. **11** Whoever speaks must do so as one speaking the very words of God; whoever serves must do so with the strength that God supplies, so that God may be glorified in all things through Jesus Christ. To Him belong the glory and power forever and ever. Amen

**Invite group members to respond to the questions printed below. If time is limited, choose the questions that best meet your group's needs:**

1. In 1Peter 4:10-11 the term "gifts" refers to abilities such as speaking and serving. What are some other gifts that God gives to people?

2. What specific gifts do you possess? (It might be easier for some group members to point out the gifts of others. You may offer this as an option.)

3. In what ways do the gifts God has given you contribute to our group's work?

4. In what ways does God strengthen us for service?

## Closing prayer

**Tell group members that you will be offering a prayer in which they will be asked to name some of the gifts that group members possess. Then pray the following prayer aloud:**

*Giving God, you have blessed our group with many gifts, including those we name before you either aloud or silently in our hearts . . . (pause). Guide us to use these gifts to serve you. Amen*

## Community Builder 7

# Using Our Gifts to Work Together

## Opening prayer

**Pray the following prayer aloud:**

Jesus our hope, you have gifted us in various ways. We come from different backgrounds. We bring to this group our unique ideas and dreams. Unite our work and our wills as one in you. Amen

## Gathering time

**Ask each person in the group to respond to one of the following:**

■ What attributes do you most admire in others? Why?

■ Tell about one of your favorite teachers.

■ Tell about a major project you completed with the help of another.

## Biblical reflection

**Read this paragraph to the group:**

In this passage from Romans, Paul defines the Christian community as the body of Christ. The Christians in the church in Rome came from different religious and social backgrounds and sometimes argued because of their differences. Paul instructs the Christians in Rome that their different talents and abilities, given to them by God, benefit the body of Christ.

**Have someone read this passage aloud:**

Romans 12:4-8:
⁴For as in one body we have many members, and not all the members have the same function, ⁵so we, who are many, are one body in Christ, and individually we are members one of another. ⁶We have gifts that differ according to the grace given to us: prophecy, in proportion to faith; ⁷ministry, in ministering; the teacher, in teaching; ⁸the exhorter, in exhortation; the giver, in generosity; the leader, in diligence; the compassionate, in cheerfulness.

**Invite group members to respond to the questions printed below. If time is limited, choose the questions that best meet your group's needs:**

1. Why was it important for the Christians in Rome to understand that God gives different types of gifts to different people?

2. If you have not completed Community Builder 6, consider together the gifts that God has given to each member of your group.

3. In what ways do the unique gifts of our group members help us to work together as a group?

4. How can we better acknowledge and celebrate the variety of gifts in our group?

## Closing prayer

**Ask each person to thank God for the gift of the person on his or her right, saying:**

*Giving God, we praise you for the gift of (name), by his/her presence you have blessed our community.*

**It might be helpful to post this prayer on a chalkboard or newsprint.**

## Community Builder 8

# Considering Our Mission

## Opening prayer

**Pray the following prayer aloud:**

Christ, our prophet, as you sent forth your first followers with the mission of making disciples, you have called us to serve. Send us into our communities to proclaim the good news that you are with us always. Amen

## Gathering time

**Ask each person in the group to respond to one of the following:**

■ Share a memorable baptism you witnessed or tell about your own.

■ Tell about someone whom you admire for their commitment to a cause or idea.

■ Tell about a time when you made and kept a promise.

## Biblical reflection

**Read this paragraph to the group:**

In Matthew's Gospel, Jesus frequently teaches about life in God's community. This passage, recording Jesus' final instructions to his disciples, occurs almost immediately following Jesus' first resurrection appearance. Jesus had gathered his remaining eleven disciples on a mountain in Galilee, where some worshiped him and others doubted (Matthew 28:17).

**Have someone read this passage aloud:**

Matthew 28:18-20:
¹⁸And Jesus came and said to them, "All authority in heaven and on earth has been given to me. ¹⁹Go therefore and make disciples of all nations, baptizing them in the name of the Father and of the Son and of the Holy Spirit, ²⁰and teaching them to obey everything that I have commanded you. And remember, I am with you always, to the end of the age."

**Invite group members to respond to the questions printed below. If time is limited, choose the questions that best meet your group's needs:**

1. What do you think it means "to make disciples of all nations"?

2. In what ways is our group currently fulfilling Jesus' commands both to make disciples and to teach others?

3. Describe in one sentence your personal mission (your reason for being on this earth).

4. How would you define our group's mission?

## Closing prayer

**Tell group members that you will be offering a prayer in which they will be invited to name some of the group's current or future projects. After each project is named, group members will pray in unison:**

*Jesus, be with us as you have promised.*

**It might be helpful to post this prayer on a chalkboard or newsprint. Begin the prayer by saying:**

*Jesus, our leader, we name before you our group's current and future tasks and projects and ask for your blessing upon them . . . (pause).*

## Community Builder 9

# Thinking about Our Group's Future

## Opening prayer

**Read the following prayer aloud:**

God of our past and future, we confess that we sometimes worry needlessly. Remind us that you will continue to protect us and provide for us in the future just as you have in the past. Amen

## Gathering time

**Ask each person in the group to respond to one of the following:**

■ Tell about a New Year's resolution you have made more than once. What makes it difficult to keep?

■ Tell about a time you worried needlessly.

■ Share a humorous experience with clothing.

## Biblical reflection

**Read this paragraph to the group:**

The sermon on the mount, chapters 5–7 of Matthew's Gospel, compiles Jesus' teaching about what it means to live in the community of faith. In the sermon on the mount, Jesus discussed the topics of anger, prayer, love, piety, and God's care for humanity.

**Have someone read this passage aloud:**

Matthew 6:25-30:
[Jesus said,] 25"Therefore I tell you, do not worry about your life, what you will eat or what you will drink, or about your body,

what you will wear. Is not life more than food, and the body more than clothing? **26**Look at the birds of the air; they neither sow nor reap nor gather into barns, and yet your heavenly Father feeds them. Are you not of more value than they? **27**And can any of you by worrying add a single hour to your span of life? **28**And why do you worry about clothing? Consider the lilies of the field, how they grow; they neither toil nor spin, **29**yet I tell you, even Solomon in all his glory was not clothed like one of these. **30**But if God so clothes the grass of the field, which is alive today and tomorrow is thrown into the oven, will he not much more clothe you—you of little faith?"

**Invite group members to respond to the questions printed below. If time is limited, choose the questions that best meet your group's needs:**

1. Jesus spoke words that both challenged and comforted his hearers. How does this passage both challenge and comfort you?

2. What challenges or worries does our group face both in doing its current work and in thinking about the future?

3. What message does this passage give to our group as we consider the future?

4. In what new directions is God calling our group?

## Closing prayer

**Tell group members that you will be offering a prayer in which they will be invited to name concerns that worry them as they look to the future— either in the group or in their personal lives. Then, pray the following prayer aloud:**

*God, our shelter, hear the concerns we name before you, both aloud and silently in our hearts . . . (pause).*

**Conclude by praying aloud:**

*God, our protector, we lay our concerns before you, trusting that whatever the future brings you will provide us with what we need. Amen*

## Community Builder 10

# Setting Goals

## Opening prayer

**Pray the following prayer aloud:**

God of the dreamers, we thank you for giving us the ability to imagine the future. Journey with us as we plan and direct each step we take toward fulfilling the visions you have planted inside us. Amen

## Gathering time

**Ask each person in the group to respond to one of the following:**

■ Tell about something you really want to do but you have been afraid to try.

■ Share one of your favorite proverbs and tell why you find it meaningful.

■ Tell about a goal you set and achieved.

## Biblical reflection

**Read this paragraph to the group:**

The book of Proverbs is intended to help the reader discern right from wrong. The book of Proverbs collects practical advice written to encourage the people of Israel to live more fruitful lives. Typically, the book consists of short statements such as the passage that follows.

**Have someone read this passage aloud:**

Proverbs 16:9:
⁹The human mind plans the way, but the LORD directs the steps.

**Invite group members to respond to the questions printed below. If time is limited, choose the questions that best meet your group's needs:**

1. What does this passage say about setting goals?

2. Recall a past task that our group set out to achieve and has accomplished. What enabled us to achieve our goal?

3. In what ways did we experience God's guidance as we worked to achieve that goal?

4. In the past, what has prevented our group from meeting its goals?

5. What three tasks would you like our group to accomplish in the coming year?

## Closing prayer

**Tell group members that you will be offering a prayer in which they will be asked to name the goals you have considered together. Begin by praying aloud:**

*Let us pray for all our goals and dreams . . .*

**After all have been named, ask the group to pray together:**

*God of goals and visions, direct our steps!*

**It might be helpful to post this prayer on a chalkboard or newsprint.**

## Community Builder 11

# Beginning a New Project

## Opening prayer

**Pray the following prayer aloud:**

God who is with us always, as you called Moses to lead the Israelites out of Egypt, you have chosen us to begin a new project. Lead us onward, watch over us, and listen when we call to you. Amen

## Gathering time

**Ask each person in the group to respond to one of the following:**

■ Tell about your first experience driving a car.

■ Describe a memorable first day of school.

■ Describe a memory of traveling alone for the first time.

## Biblical reflection

**Read this paragraph to the group:**

At the time God spoke to Moses, the people of Israel were enslaved in Egypt. Moses, an Israelite by birth, was raised by the daughter of Pharaoh. God chose Moses to help lead the Israelites out of slavery. This passage has three central components: God's call to Moses, Moses' resistant response, and God's promise to be with Moses as he fulfills God's call.

**Have someone read this passage aloud:**

Exodus 3:10-12:

[God said to Moses,] **10** "So come, I will send you to Pharaoh to bring my people, the Israelites, out of Egypt." **11**But Moses said to God, "Who am I that I should go to Pharaoh, and bring the Israelites out of Egypt?" **12**He said, "I will be with you; and this shall be the sign for you that it is I who sent you: when you have brought the people out of Egypt, you shall worship God on this mountain."

**Invite group members to respond to the questions printed below. If time is limited, choose the questions that best meet your group's needs:**

1. Had you been Moses, how would you have responded to God's call?

2. What are you hesitant about as our group considers beginning a new project?

3. What about our new project excites you?

4. In what ways can God's words, "I will be with you," inspire and motivate us as we go about our group's work?

# Closing prayer

**Conclude by praying aloud:**

*Ever-present God, as you once promised Moses, "I will be with you," accompany us as we move forward, taking on new tasks to better serve you. Amen*

## Community Builder 12

# Making God Our First Priority

## Opening prayer

**Pray the following prayer aloud:**

Eternal God, as we work together, renew our love for you. Strengthen the faith in our hearts and souls and enlighten our minds with your word. Amen

## Gathering time

**Ask each person in the group to respond to one of the following:**

■ What is one activity or hobby you would have a difficult time giving up? Why?

■ If you could ask Jesus one question, what would it be and why?

■ Tell about a challenging experience with a neighbor.

## Biblical reflection

**Read this paragraph to the group:**

Immediately following Jesus' triumphant entry into Jerusalem, the religious leaders confronted Jesus with challenges and questions, concluding with this often debated one, "Which commandment is the first of all?" Jesus' answer echoes Moses' message to the people of Israel (see Deuteronomy 6:4-5), commanding them to choose the God of Israel and cast away all other gods.

① xerusartsfaction

※ Nora Edie mode

※ AriL Martins - jolce home

※ Mariah Canty, common

**Have someone read this passage aloud:**

Mark 12:28-31:
**28** One of the scribes came near and heard them disputing with one another, and seeing that [Jesus] answered them well, he asked him, "Which commandment is the first of all?" **29** Jesus answered, "The first is, 'Hear, O Israel: the Lord our God, the Lord is one; **30**you shall love the Lord your God with all your heart, and with all your soul, and with all your mind, and with all your strength.' **31**The second is this, 'You shall love your neighbor as yourself.' There is no other commandment greater than these."

**Invite group members to respond to the questions printed below. If time is limited, choose the questions that best meet your group's needs:**

1. What are some concrete ways in which Christians seek to love God with all their "heart . . . and soul . . . and mind . . . and strength"?

2. In most Christians' lives, what do you think competes with God for their love and attention?

3. In what ways does our group struggle to keep God as the first priority in our work?

4. What actions can our group take to help us keep God as our first priority?

## Closing prayer

**Tell group members that during the prayer they will be asked to name silently some of the things that compete with God to be their first priority. Begin by praying:**

*Holy Trinity, One God, we are tempted to give other things priority over you . . . (pause) .*

**Conclude by praying:**

*Help us to love you first of all, help us to love you most of all, help us to love you with all of our heart and soul and mind and strength. Amen*

## Community Builder 13

# Following Jesus in Our Work

## Opening prayer

**Instruct the group that each time the leader says, "When we hear you calling, Jesus," the group will respond, "Inspire us to follow."**

Leader:     When we hear you calling, Jesus,

Group:      Inspire us to follow.

Leader:     You have called us to be fishers of people. When we hear you calling, Jesus,

Group:      Inspire us to follow.

Leader:     You have called us to serve you through the work of our group. When we hear you calling, Jesus,

Group:      Inspire us to follow.

## Gathering time

**Ask each person in the group to respond to one of the following:**

■ Describe something you learned to do by following the example of someone else.

■ Share a fishing story.

■ Tell about one of the most impulsive things you have ever done.

## Biblical reflection

**Read this paragraph to the group:**

In Mark's Gospel this passage describes Jesus' first act of ministry after his baptism and temptation. When Jesus invited Simon and

Andrew to follow him, the brothers became the first of Jesus' twelve disciples. Throughout the Gospels Jesus invited a variety of people to follow him, often those on the fringes of society.

**Have someone read this passage aloud:**

Mark 1:16-18:
[16]As Jesus passed along the Sea of Galilee, he saw Simon and his brother Andrew casting a net into the sea—for they were fishermen. [17]And Jesus said to them, "Follow me and I will make you fish for people." [18]And immediately they left their nets and followed him.

**Invite group members to respond to the questions printed below. If time is limited, choose the questions that best meet your group's needs:**

1. What do you think are the characteristics of a follower of Jesus?

2. Tell about an experience that illustrates what type of follower you are: impulsive like Andrew and Peter, slow and deliberate, or somewhere in between.

3. How do our different ways of following Jesus help us to work together as a group?

4. What does it mean to be "fishers of people"?

5. In what ways does our group serve as "fishers of people"?

## Closing prayer

**Invite group members to pray for ministries in the congregation and community by completing the following prayer sentence:**

*Jesus, bless our ministry of _____.*

**When all have finished, conclude by praying together:**

*Jesus, make us all fishers of people. Amen*

**It might be helpful to write these prayer sentences on a chalkboard or newsprint.**

## Community Builder 14

# Being Leaders Who Serve Others

## Opening prayer

**Pray the following prayer aloud:**

Humble Jesus, helper of the weak, as we minister through our work, remind us that you have called us to follow your example of serving others. Amen

## Gathering time

**Ask each person in the group to respond to one of the following:**

■ Tell about a time when you were sick and someone took care of you.

■ Tell about a time when you served another and received an unexpected blessing.

■ Tell about a humorous dining experience.

## Biblical reflection

**Read this paragraph to the group:**

According to Luke's Gospel, a dispute arose in the middle of Jesus' last supper with his disciples. The disciples argued about which one among them could be considered the greatest. Jesus' teaching about servanthood reflects his actions of caring for those who were poor and outcast.

**Have someone read this passage aloud:**

Luke 22:25-27:
**25** But [Jesus] said to them, "The kings of the Gentiles lord it over them; and those in authority over them are called benefactors. **26**But not so with you; rather the greatest among you must become like the youngest, and the leader like one who serves. **27**For who is greater, the one who is at the table or the one who serves? Is it not the one at the table? But I am among you as one who serves."

**Invite group members to respond to the questions printed below. If time is limited, choose the questions that best meet your group's needs:**

1. In what ways do you think of Jesus as being one who served others?

2. Why are Jesus' words in Luke 22:25-27 important for our group to hear, even though we may not think of ourselves as having authority?

3. In what ways is God calling us, through our work, to be leaders in this congregation?

4. What are some of the ways that we, as leaders, can serve others through our group's work?

## Closing prayer

**Tell group members that you will be offering a prayer in which they will be asked to name some of the tasks that the group does. At the appropriate time in the prayer, they can name these tasks either aloud or silently in their hearts. Begin by praying:**

*Gentle God, we serve you and others through these tasks . . . (pause).*

**Conclude by praying in unison:**

*Gentle God, help us to be leaders who serve others.*

**It might be helpful to post this prayer sentence on a chalkboard or newsprint.**

| Community Builder 15 | # Being Leaders Who Guide Others |
|---|---|

## Opening prayer

**Instruct the group that each time the leader says, "Jesus, light of the world," the group will respond, "Let your light shine upon us."**

Leader:     We gather as children of God. Jesus, light of the world,

Group:     Let your light shine upon us.

Leader:     Warm us with your words of hope. Jesus, light of the world,

Group:     Let your light shine upon us.

Leader:     Ignite in us the yearning to lead others to you. Jesus, light of the world,

Group:     Let your light shine upon us.

## Gathering time

**Ask each person in the group to respond to one of the following:**

■ Describe a time when you saw a glorious sunrise or sunset.

■ Tell about a time when the lights went out.

■ Tell about an experience with candles or fire.

## Biblical reflection

**Read this paragraph to the group:**

In John's Gospel, Jesus describes himself as "the light of the world." In this passage, from Matthew's account of Jesus' sermon on the mount, Jesus commands his followers to share in the task of reflecting God's love in their words and actions.

**Have someone read this passage aloud:**

Matthew 5:14-16:
[Jesus said,] **14**"You are the light of the world. A city built on a hill cannot be hid. **15**No one after lighting a lamp puts it under the bushel basket, but on the lampstand, and it gives light to all in the house. **16**In the same way, let your light shine before others, so that they may see your good works and give glory to your Father in heaven."

**Invite group members to respond to the questions printed below. If time is limited, choose the questions that best meet your group's needs:**

1. Why is the image of shining as a light an especially important description of what Christian leaders do?

2. In what ways can or does our group's work guide others and give glory to God?

3. What are ways in which Christians might hide their lights under the bushel basket?

4. What are some ways that our group is currently "hiding its light"? What can we do to "let the light shine"?

## Closing prayer

**Ask group members to pray for the person on their right, saying to them in turn:**

*(Name), you are a light of the world.*

**When all have been prayed for, pray aloud:**

*Almighty God, sun of righteousness, you have filled us with the new light of your Son, Jesus Christ. Let the light of our faith shine in all that we do. In Jesus' name, Amen*

## Community Builder 16

# Serving God in All We Do

## Opening prayer

**Pray the following prayer aloud:**

Jesus, Lord of the vineyard, plant in us the desire to faithfully serve you, no matter how small or large the task. Amen

## Gathering time

**Ask each person in the group to respond to one of the following:**

■ Tell about one of your first jobs.

■ Describe a time when you were honest even though it was difficult.

■ Describe the most fulfilling part of your daily work or routine.

## Biblical reflection

**Read this paragraph to the group:**

In Jesus' parable of the dishonest manager, he uses the saying in Luke 16:10 to highlight the meaning of the story. In the parable, a manager—in order to clear his reputation for the future—settled his accounts and won the favor of his employer. Jesus presents several explanations of the parable, including this one which encourages followers to serve God in every aspect of their lives.

**Have someone read this passage aloud:**

Luke 16:10:
[Jesus said,] **10**"Whoever is faithful in a very little is faithful also in much; and whoever is dishonest in a very little is dishonest also in much."

**Invite group members to respond to the questions printed below. If time is limited, choose the questions that best meet your group's needs:**

1. In this text, what is Jesus asking of the hearer?

2. From your own experience, share some examples that illustrate Jesus' message in Luke 16:10. (It might be helpful to read the text again.)

3. What are the small and large tasks that our group does?

4. In what ways are the small tasks that our group does significant?

5. How can we better acknowledge the small tasks that each of us does (both in the group and in the congregation)?

## Closing prayer

**Ask each group member to pray for the person on his or her right by saying:**

*I pray for (name), that he/she may be a faithful servant of God.*

**It might be helpful to post this prayer on a chalkboard or newsprint.**

| Community Builder 17 | # Making the Best Use of Our Resources |
| --- | --- |

## Opening prayer

**Instruct the group that each time the leader says, "We pray," the group will respond, "Help us to be content."**

Leader:     God of both little and plenty, we pray,

Group:      Help us to be content.

Leader:     God of the hungry and well fed, we pray,

Group:      Help us to be content.

Leader:     In any and all circumstances, we pray,

Group:      Help us to be content.

## Gathering time

**Ask each person in the group to respond to one of the following:**

■ Tell about a time when you needed to be resourceful.

■ Tell about a time that you bought something you really didn't need.

■ Tell about a free or inexpensive activity you enjoy.

## Biblical reflection

**Read this paragraph to the group:**

Paul wrote to the beloved people of Philippi from prison. In this passage, he thanks the Philippians for the gift of money they sent to help him. Paul reminds the Philippians that he has learned to be content in every situation and consequently does not depend on their gifts.

**Have someone read this passage aloud:**

Philippians 4:11b-13:

**11b** . . . for I have learned to be content with whatever I have. **12**I know what it is to have little, and I know what it is to have plenty. In any and all circumstances I have learned the secret of being well-fed and of going hungry, of having plenty and of being in need. **13**I can do all things through him who strengthens me.

**Invite group members to respond to the questions printed below. If time is limited, choose the questions that best meet your group's needs:**

1. Tell about someone whose life illustrates Paul's philosophy of being content in all circumstances.

2. Paul managed to proclaim the gospel despite limited resources. Resources can be defined as money, time, abilities, and the support of others. How can making the best use of one's resources be a way of serving God?

3. What are the resources that help our group do its work?

4. What resources are we lacking?

5. What can we do to meet our needs for the resources we lack?

## Closing prayer

**Ask each person to pray for the group member on his or her right by saying:**

*God of power and might, remind (name) that she/he can do all things through Christ who strengthens her/him.*

**It might be helpful to post this prayer on a chalkboard or newsprint.**

## Community Builder 18

# Helping Those in Need

## Opening prayer

**Pray the following prayer aloud:**

Jesus, living bread from heaven, feed our hungry spirits and quench our thirst for you. Awaken in us the desire to care for others and motivate us to share our blessings with those in need. Amen

## Gathering time

**Ask each person in the group to respond to one of the following:**

■ Share a gardening story.

■ Tell about a time when you desired something you couldn't afford.

■ If you had five thousand dollars to give to a charity, which would you choose and why?

## Biblical reflection

**Read this paragraph to the group:**

Throughout their history, God called the people of Israel to care for those in need—strangers, poor people, widows, and orphans. The prophet Isaiah challenged the people of Israel to share their resources with others. He promised them that their good deeds would be rewarded. In the New Testament, Jesus ministered to many who were neglected by society and encouraged his followers to do the same.

Isaiah 58:10-11:
**10**If you offer your food to the hungry and satisfy the needs of the afflicted, then your light shall rise in the darkness and your gloom be like the noonday. **11**The LORD will guide you continually, and satisfy your needs in parched places, and make your bones strong; and you shall be like a watered garden, like a spring of water, whose waters never fail.

**Invite group members to respond to the questions printed below. If time is limited, choose the questions that best meet your group's needs:**

1. In this text, what does the prophet Isaiah ask of and promise to the hearer?

2. In our congregation and community, who are those in need?

3. In what ways does our group's work help those in need?

4. What are the blessings our group has received when we have helped others?

## Closing prayer

**Tell group members that you will be offering a prayer in which they will be asked to name congregational ministries and community groups in need of help. For example, this could include a food pantry, a domestic abuse shelter, or a literacy program. After each ministry or group is mentioned, invite the group to respond in unison:**

*Jesus, bless all who serve.*

**Begin by praying:**

*We pray for the work of all who help those in need, including those we name before you now . . . (pause).*

## Community Builder 19

# Sharing Our Faith with Others

## Opening prayer

**Pray the following prayer aloud:**

God of both light and darkness, we praise you for choosing us to be your people. Stretch our lives beyond the familiar boundaries and prod us to proclaim the stories of your mighty acts to all who will hear. Amen

## Gathering time

**Ask each person in the group to respond to one of the following:**

■ Tell about a time when someone shared his or her faith with you.

■ With whom do you feel most comfortable talking about your faith and why?

■ Tell about a time you lent a valuable or meaningful possession to another.

## Biblical reflection

**Read this paragraph to the group:**

The First Letter of Peter was written to Christians experiencing persecution. In this section, the writer encourages the hearers to concentrate on living holy lives. This passage uses phrases from the Old Testament, originally applied to the Israelites, to speak about Christians—chosen race, royal priesthood, and holy nation.

**Have someone read this passage aloud:**

1 Peter 2:9:
⁹But you are a chosen race, a royal priesthood, a holy nation, God's own people, in order that you may proclaim the mighty acts of him who called you out of darkness into his marvelous light.

**Invite group members to respond to the questions printed below. If time is limited, choose the questions that best meet your group's needs:**

1. What do you find difficult about sharing your faith?

2. According to 1 Peter 2:9, what makes us qualified to share the Christian faith with others?

3. In what ways does our group's work proclaim the gospel to others?

4. In what ways could our group be more intentional about sharing our Christian faith with others through our work?

## Closing prayer

**Tell group members that you will be closing with a few minutes of silent prayer. Ask them to use that time to name others with whom they could share their Christian faith.**

**Community Builder 20**

# Expanding Our Group

## Opening prayer

**Pray the following prayer aloud:**

God of strangers and friends, throughout history you have visited your people. Release our hearts and minds from prejudice and fear so that we may not miss you when you come to us. Amen

## Gathering time

**Ask each person in the group to respond to one of the following:**

■ Describe a positive experience you have had with a stranger.

■ If you could entertain three guests at your home, who would you invite and why?

■ Tell about an encounter with someone who spoke a different language.

## Biblical reflection

**Read this paragraph to the group:**

In the desert land where Abraham and Sarah lived, residents were expected to extend hospitality to visitors. The writer of Hebrews, who used this story to encourage Christians to welcome strangers, wrote, "Do not neglect to show hospitality to strangers, for by doing that some have entertained angels without knowing it" (Hebrews 13:2).

**Have someone read this passage aloud:**

Genesis 18:1-4:

¹The LORD appeared to Abraham by the oaks of Mamre, as he sat at the entrance of his tent in the heat of the day. ²He looked up and saw three men standing near him. When he saw them, he ran from the tent entrance to meet them, and bowed down to the ground. ³He said, "My lord, if I find favor with you, do not pass by your servant. ⁴Let a little water be brought, and wash your feet, and rest yourselves under the tree."

**Invite group members to respond to the questions printed below. If time is limited, choose the questions that best meet your group's needs:**

1. After welcoming the three strangers, Abraham and Sarah were blessed with the news that they would become parents. What risks did Abraham and Sarah take in welcoming these strangers?

2. What are the blessings and risks our group might encounter in welcoming new members?

3. Does our group need to add new members? Why or why not?

4. If our group does need to expand, who are some of the people we could invite to be new members?

5. What concrete actions can we take to invite and welcome new people into our group?

## Closing prayer

**Begin the closing prayer by having group members describe in one sentence a recent blessing they have received from another person, either a friend or a stranger. After each blessing is named, ask the group to respond in unison:**

*Could this be the work of Christ among us?*

**Conclude by praying aloud:**

*Surprising God, we thank you for the many blessings you have showered upon us. Amen*

## Community Builder 21
# Receiving God's Unconditional Love

## Opening prayer

**Pray the following prayer aloud:**

O God of all goodness and love, open our eyes that we may see your blessings. Open our minds that we may accept your grace. Open our hearts that we may not fear sharing your love. Amen

## Gathering time

**Ask each person in the group to respond to one of the following:**

- Tell about a time you showed unconditional love for another.

- What do you think heaven will be like?

- Tell about something you have saved from your childhood that is meaningful to you.

## Biblical reflection

**Read this paragraph to the group:**

This passage records one of the apostle Paul's central teachings— that through Christ, God loves us, forgives us, and gives us eternal life as free gifts. As Christians, we need only believe to receive these blessings.

**Have someone read this passage aloud:**

Ephesians 2:4-9:
⁴But God, who is rich in mercy, out of the great love with which he loved us ⁵even when we were dead through our trespasses, made us alive together with Christ—by grace you have been saved—⁶and raised us up with him and seated us with him in the heavenly places in Christ Jesus, ⁷so that in the ages to come he might show the immeasurable riches of his grace in kindness toward us in Christ Jesus. ⁸For by grace you have been saved through faith, and this is not your own doing; it is the gift of God—⁹not the result of works, so that no one may boast.

**Invite group members to respond to the questions printed below. If time is limited, choose the questions that best meet your group's needs:**

1. What are some examples of both conditional and unconditional love?

2. In what ways has our group experienced God's unconditional love?

3. According to the text, good works do not earn God's love. What motivates you, as a member of this group, to do good works?

4. How does knowing that God loves us unconditionally help our group in doing its tasks?

## Closing prayer

**Tell the group that you will be using a sentence prayer. Ask group members to complete the sentence:**

*We thank you for _____.*

**Not every person needs to answer and those who wish to may answer more than once. Begin by praying:**

*Gracious and merciful God, we thank you for _____.*

<table>
<tr><td>**Community Builder 22**</td><td># Receiving God's Peace</td></tr>
</table>

## Opening prayer

**Pray the following prayer aloud:**

Jesus, our protector, like your first disciples, we sometimes become burdened by the worries of this world. Embrace us with your peaceful spirit and set our troubled hearts at rest. Amen

## Gathering time

**Ask each person in the group to respond to one of the following:**

- Tell about one of your childhood fears.
- What one thing do you think most people are worried about? Why?
- Describe one of your favorite peaceful places.

## Biblical reflection

**Read this paragraph to the group:**

Jesus spoke the words recorded in John 14:27 to his disciples at his last meal with them. He had just promised his followers that he would send his Holy Spirit to guide and teach them. At the end of the meal, Jesus was arrested, tried, and put to death.

**Have someone read this passage aloud:**

John 14:27:
²⁷Peace I leave with you; my peace I give to you. I do not give to you as the world gives. Do not let your hearts be troubled, and do not let them be afraid.

**Invite group members to respond to the questions printed below. If time is limited, choose the questions that best meet your group's needs:**

1. How does the peace that Jesus gives differ from "worldly" peace?

2. When has our group needed to hear Jesus' words about peace?

3. What are the fears that currently trouble our group?

4. Tell about a time that you, alone or as a part of this group, experienced the peace that Jesus talks about.

## Closing prayer

**Invite group members to complete the following sentence prayer petition:**

*Jesus, sometimes we fear _____.*

**As a group, respond to each petition by praying together:**

*Jesus, give us your peace.*

It might be helpful to post these prayer sentences on chalkboard or newsprint.

## Community Builder 23

# Receiving God's Strength

## Opening prayer

**Instruct the group that each time the leader says, "You give power to the faint," the group will respond, "And strength to the powerless."**

Leader:      We worship you, life-giving God. You give power to the faint,

Group:      And strength to the powerless.

Leader:      We worship you for lifting us up when we are weary. You give power to the faint,

Group:      And strength to the powerless.

Leader:      We worship you for renewing our hope. You give power to the faint,

Group:      And strength to the powerless.

## Gathering time

**Ask each person in the group to respond to one of the following:**

■ Tell about an experience that required your physical strength and endurance.

■ Tell about an experience on an airplane.

■ Tell about a time when you felt totally exhausted but needed to keep going.

## Biblical reflection

**Read this paragraph to the group:**

Isaiah 40 was written to the Israelites who were living in exile in Babylon in the sixth century B.C. The hymn in Isaiah 40:12-21 celebrated God's glory and denounced the existence of other gods. The writer asserts that the God of Israel created the world and has the power and compassion to save the people of Israel.

**Have someone read this passage aloud:**

Isaiah 40:29-31:
[29][God] gives power to the faint, and strengthens the powerless. [30]Even youths will faint and be weary, and the young will fall exhausted; [31]but those who wait for the LORD shall renew their strength, they shall mount up with wings like eagles, they shall run and not be weary, they shall walk and not faint.

**Invite group members to respond to the questions printed below. If time is limited, choose the questions that best meet your group's needs:**

1. What do you think Isaiah means by the phrase, "those who wait for the LORD will renew their strength"?

2. What do you find most exhausting about our group's work?

3. In the past when has God's strength enabled our group to complete tasks despite our weariness?

4. For what situations do we group currently need God's strength?

## Closing prayer

**Tell group members that you will be offering a prayer during which they are encouraged to name silently before God aspects of your group's work that they find tiring. Begin by praying:**

*God, hearer of those who call on you, we silently name before you the tasks and duties which, though important, tire us . . . (pause).*

**When two or three minutes have passed, pray:**

*All powerful God, renew our strength. Amen*

## Community Builder 24

# Receiving God's Wisdom

## Opening prayer

**Pray the following prayer aloud:**

God of wisdom, shine your truth into our minds so that we may better understand your ways. Prepare our hearts that we may gratefully receive your guidance. Amen

## Gathering time

**Ask each person in the group to respond to one of the following:**

■ What area of study did you most enjoy while you were in school and why?

■ What piece of wisdom would you want to pass on to the next generation?

■ Tell about a wise person who has inspired you.

## Biblical reflection

**Read this paragraph to the group:**

According to Paul, the Corinthian congregation took part in actions that were not appropriate for Christians. These actions included drunkenness, quarreling, and boastfulness. In this passage, Paul contrasts God's wisdom to human wisdom, reminding the congregation that their only reason to boast is Christ.

**Have someone read this passage aloud:**

1 Corinthians 1:25-31:
[25] For God's foolishness is wiser than human wisdom, and God's weakness is stronger than human strength. [26] Consider your own call, brothers and sisters: not many of you were wise by human standards, not many were powerful, not many were of noble birth. [27] But God chose what is foolish in the world to shame the wise; God chose what is weak in the world to shame the strong; [28] God chose what is low and despised in the world, things that are not, to reduce to nothing things that are, [29] so that no one might boast in the presence of God. [30] He is the source of your life in Christ Jesus, who became for us wisdom from God, and right-eousness and sanctification and redemption, [31] in order that, as it is written, "Let the one who boasts, boast in the Lord."

**Invite group members to respond to the questions printed below. If time is limited, choose the questions that best meet your group's needs:**

1. What is wisdom and why does our group need it for our work?

2. In your life, where have you seen that God's foolishness is wiser than human wisdom?

3. In our group's work, where or to whom do we turn to find wisdom?

4. What pieces of wisdom have you learned from your work in this group?

## Closing prayer

**Discuss together your prayer concerns. Remind group members that each time they mention a prayer concern, God hears it as a prayer. When you have finished raising your concerns, close with silent prayer asking for God's wisdom and guidance.**

## Community Builder 25

# Receiving Guidance through Scripture

## Opening prayer

**Pray the following prayer aloud:**

Great and glorious God, your word shines out to guide us when we cannot see the path, brings sweetness to soothe us when our lives are bitter, and provides clarity when we become confused. Renew daily our delight in your Word. Amen

## Gathering time

**Ask each person in the group to respond to one of the following:**

■ What is your favorite book and why?

■ Describe a humorous experience in a library.

■ What are the sweetest words anyone has ever spoken to you?

## Biblical reflection

**Read this paragraph to the group:**

Psalm 119, the longest psalm in the Bible, praises God for the gift of the Law. The psalmist understood God's law to be the Pentateuch (the first five books of the Bible). This psalm is also a wisdom poem, teaching the reader about right and wrong. The psalmist celebrates God's law as both a comfort and a guide for life.

**Have someone read this passage aloud:**

Psalm 119:103-105:
[103]How sweet are your words to my taste, sweeter than honey to my mouth! [104]Through your precepts I get understanding; therefore I hate every false way. [105]Your word is a lamp to my feet and a light to my path.

**Invite group members to respond to the questions printed below. If time is limited, choose the questions that best meet your group's needs.**

1. The psalmist uses images involving the senses of sight and taste to describe God's word. How would you describe God's word using images drawn from the other senses? (God's word sounds like, smells like, or feels like _____.)

2. What are some of the Scripture passages you remember or most treasure?

3. Could any of these Scripture passages provide guidance for our group as we work? If so, which ones and why?

4. God speaks to Christians through the Scriptures. What other ways does God speak to our group today?

## Closing prayer

**Tell group members that you will be offering a sentence prayer in which they will be asked to name the ways in which the Scriptures help them in their lives. Begin by praying:**

*Your word brings us _____.*

**Conclude by praying aloud:**

*Providing God, we bless and praise you for the gift of your word, which has sustained us in many ways. In the name of your Son, Jesus, we pray. Amen*

## Community Builder 26

# Receiving Guidance through Prayer

## Opening prayer

**Instruct the group that each time the leader says, "Guiding God," the group will respond, "Remind us to pray."**

Leader: Ever-present God, we praise you for hearing our prayers and concerns. When we are thankful, guiding God,

Group: Remind us to pray.

Leader: When we are worried, guiding God,

Group: Remind us to pray.

Leader: When we seek direction, guiding God,

Group: Remind us to pray.

Leader: In all times and places, guiding God,

Group: Remind us to pray.

## Gathering time

**Ask each person in the group to respond to one of the following:**

■ Tell about something you asked for and didn't receive.

■ Describe a memorable Thanksgiving Day.

■ Tell about something that causes you stress.

# Biblical reflection

**Read this paragraph to the group:**

While he was in prison, Paul wrote to the Philippians. Despite his life's difficult circumstances, Paul was able to encourage Christians to rejoice in their faith and trust God in all situations. Paul began his letter by reminding the Philippians that he prays with thankfulness to God for them. In this passage, he encourages the people of Philippi to ask God for what they need.

**Have someone read this passage aloud:**

Philippians 4:6-7:
⁶Do not worry about anything, but in everything by prayer and supplication with thanksgiving let your requests be made known to God. ⁷And the peace of God, which surpasses all understanding, will guard your hearts and your minds in Christ Jesus.

**Invite group members to respond to the questions printed below. If time is limited, choose the questions that best meet your group's needs:**

1. Paul says that through prayer, Christians receive God's peace. How has prayer helped you in your life?

2. What prevents people from praying?

3. What would you say to someone who said, "We have too much to do—we don't have time to pray in our group meetings"?

4. For what does our group most need to pray as we do our work?

# Closing prayer

**Invite group members to voice their prayer concerns. After each name or concern is mentioned, ask them to respond:**

*Jesus, hear our prayer.*

## Community Builder 27

# Receiving Guidance through Worship

## Opening prayer

**Pray the following prayer aloud:**

Shepherding God, we thank you for bringing us together to hear your word, sing your praises, and reach out to you in prayer. As we gather in your name, reveal to us your vision for our work and prepare our hearts for serving you. Amen

## Gathering time

**Ask each person in the group to respond to one of the following:**

■ Describe a unique or meaningful worship service you attended.

■ What is your favorite hymn and why?

■ What part of the worship experience do you find most inspirational and why?

## Biblical reflection

**Read this paragraph to the group:**

This psalm of praise was written as a call to worship the God of Israel, who had done marvelous things for the people. The Bible presents many ways of understanding both God and the community of faith. This psalm uses the popular biblical image of God as the shepherd and the believers as the "people of [God's] pasture."

**Have someone read this passage aloud:**

Psalm 95:6-7:
[6]O come, let us worship and bow down, let us kneel before the LORD, our Maker! [7]For he is our God, and we are the people of his pasture, and the sheep of his hand. O that today you would listen to his voice!

**Invite group members to respond to the questions printed below. If time is limited, choose the questions that best meet your group's needs:**

1. What motivates you to attend worship?

2. What would you say to someone who said, "I don't need to worship. I praise God by serving on this committee"?

3. How does our group's work relate to or enhance the church's worship experiences?

4. In what ways does worship guide, inspire, or encourage our group in its work?

## Closing prayer

**Tell group members that you will be offering a prayer in which they will be asked to name the people who plan, lead, and assist with the worship services in your congregation. Begin by praying:**

*God, our creator, we name before you, both aloud and silently, those people who help to plan and lead worship . . . (pause).*

**Conclude by praying:**

*God our maker, with gratitude we honor the service of these people. Through their leadership you draw our hearts and minds to you. Bless their work and ours. Amen*

## Community Builder 28
# Receiving Guidance through Others

## Opening prayer

**Pray the following prayer aloud:**

God of all times and places, you have lifted up leaders in the faith to guide and encourage us. We praise you for the powerful witness of those sisters and brothers in Christ who—with devotion and compassion—have shared their faith with us. Amen

## Gathering time

**Ask each person in the group to respond to one of the following:**

■ Tell about one of your childhood heroes.

■ Tell a story about a favorite grandparent.

■ Who in your family are you most like and why?

## Biblical reflection

**Read this paragraph to the group:**

The Second Letter of Paul to Timothy was written to instruct Timothy as a church leader. These verses remind Timothy that his belief in Christ came to him through the teaching and example of his mother and grandmother.

**Have someone read this passage aloud:**

2 Timothy 1:3-5:
[3]I am grateful to God—whom I worship with a clear conscience, as my ancestors did—when I remember you constantly in my prayers night and day. [4]Recalling your tears, I long to see you so that I may be filled with joy. [5]I am reminded of your sincere faith, a faith that lived first in your grandmother Lois and your mother Eunice and now, I am sure, lives in you.

**Invite group members to respond to the questions printed below. If time is limited, choose the questions that best meet your group's needs:**

1. How do you think being a third generation believer strengthened Timothy?

2. Who has encouraged you to serve in this group or in the congregation?

3. What generations are represented in our group? How does each of these generations influence and inspire our group's work?

4. How does our group help the congregation to pass the faith on to younger generations?

## Closing prayer

**Pray the following prayer, instructing group members to name Christians who have been important to them and the church and who have died:**

*God of all generations, we thank you for those Christians who have gone before us and especially for those we now name . . . (pause).*

**When all have finished, conclude by praying:**

*Inspire us to honor the memory of those we have named by sharing our faith with one another and with future generations. Amen*

## Community Builder 29

# Loving One Another

## Opening prayer

**Pray the following prayer aloud:**

Jesus our teacher, you have commanded us to love one another as you first loved us. Create in us the will and show us the way to love both in word and in deed. Amen

## Gathering time

**Ask each person in the group to respond to one of the following:**

- Describe a memorable Valentine's Day experience.

- Describe a memorable wedding you attended.

- Describe your first encounter with someone you love (for example, a child, a friend, or your spouse).

## Biblical reflection

**Read this paragraph to the group:**

John 13–17 records Jesus' words and actions at his last meal with his disciples and closest friends. Prior to giving this command to love one another, Jesus washed the feet of his disciples and talked about servanthood. Later, Jesus repeated this commandment to love, adding, "No one has greater love than this, to lay down one's life for one's friends" (John 15:13).

John 13:34-35:
**34**I give you a new commandment, that you love one another. Just as I have loved you, you also should love one another. **35**By this everyone will know that you are my disciples, if you have love for one another.

**Invite group members to respond to the questions printed below. If time is limited, choose the questions that best meet your group's needs:**

1. In the Gospels, how did Jesus show love to his followers?

2. In what ways do you experience Jesus' love for you?

3. One way Jesus demonstrated his love was by washing his disciples' feet. Through what concrete actions has our group demonstrated love to one another?

4. How does the work we do as a group demonstrate love to the members of our church and community?

## Closing prayer

**Tell group members that during the prayer they will be invited to name, both aloud and silently, people who have demonstrated Christian love to them. Begin by praying:**

*Loving Jesus, by your life's example you have taught us to love one another. We thank you for those who follow your example, sharing Christian love with us . . . (pause).*

## Community Builder 30

# Sharing with One Another

## Opening prayer

**Pray the following prayer aloud:**

God, source of all good things, deepen our connection with one another, so that we might be of one heart and soul. Amen

## Gathering time

**Ask each person in the group to respond to one of the following:**

■ If you could live in any period of history, when would it be? Why?

■ Tell about a possession you would be glad to get rid of.

■ Describe an experience buying or renting a home or apartment.

## Biblical reflection

**Read this paragraph to the group:**

The book of Acts, written by the same person who authored the Gospel of Luke, records the history of the early Christians. After Jesus' ascension, the Holy Spirit descended upon the first believers, marking the birth of the Christian church.

**Have someone read this passage aloud:**

Acts 4:32-35:
[32]Now the whole group of those who believed were of one heart and soul, and no one claimed private ownership of any possessions, but everything they owned was held in common. [33]With great power the apostles gave their testimony to the resurrection of the Lord Jesus, and great grace was upon them all. [34]There was not a needy person among them, for as many as owned lands or houses sold them and brought the proceeds of what was sold. [35]They laid it at the apostles' feet, and it was distributed to each as any had need.

**Invite group members to respond to the questions printed below. If time is limited, choose the questions that best meet your group's needs:**

1. What are the characteristics of the early church as described in this passage from the book of Acts?

2. Some people claim that this passage is a description of the ideal church community. Describe your concept of the ideal church.

3. What do you think it means to be of "one heart and soul"?

4. How is the group described in Acts 4:32-35 similar to and different from our group?

5. What are some of the resources that our group members can share with one another as we do our work together?

## Closing prayer

**Invite group members to take a few minutes to silently ask God to help them consider ways they can better share their own resources, abilities, and insights with other group members.**

## Community Builder 31

# Being Kind to One Another

## Opening prayer

**Pray the following prayer aloud:**

God of all kindness, surround us with your forgiving love so that we might, in turn, give grace to one another. Amen

## Gathering time

**Ask each person in the group to respond to one of the following:**

■ Tell about a childhood nickname that you disliked.

■ Describe something that you built.

■ Describe an act of kindness that you recently experienced.

## Biblical reflection

**Read this paragraph to the group:**

The book of Ephesians summarizes Paul's teachings about Christian unity. In this chapter, Paul teaches that being a Christian changes how people relate to one another. He offers specific advice for the Christian's life.

**Have someone read this passage aloud:**

Ephesians 4:29-32:
[29]Let no evil talk come out of your mouths, but only what is useful for building up, as there is need, so that your words may give grace to those who hear. [30]And do not grieve the Holy Spirit of God, with which you were marked with a seal for the day of redemption. [31]Put away from you all bitterness and wrath and anger and wrangling and slander, together with all malice, [32]and be kind to one another, tenderhearted, forgiving one another, as God in Christ has forgiven you.

**Invite group members to respond to the questions printed below. If time is limited, choose the questions that best meet your group's needs:**

1. What are some concrete ways Christians can be kind to one another?

2. When have you heard or spoken words that "gave grace" (Ephesians 4:29) to you or others?

3. What do you think it means to be "tenderhearted" (Ephesians 4:32)?

4. How well is our group doing at following the advice in Ephesians 4:29-32?

5. What kind words or acts would inspire our group as we do our work?

## Closing prayer

**Ask group members to list privately on a piece of paper any problems that could potentially cause them to feel angry or bitter. When all have finished, ask them to tear their papers into tiny shreds and throw them in a wastebasket that you have provided. Say this prayer aloud:**

*Holy Spirit, life-giver, fill our mouths with gracious words, and warm our hearts with tenderness so that we may be kind to one another. Amen*

## Community Builder 32

# Communicating with One Another

## Opening prayer

**Pray the following prayer aloud:**

Christ, the head of the body, we are knit together as one people in your name. Pour into our hearts your loving spirit so that we may speak words that promote growth and health. Amen

## Gathering time

**Ask each person in the group to respond to one of the following:**

■ Tell about a time when you had to speak in public.

■ Tell about an experience with a computer.

■ Share a humorous story about miscommunication.

## Biblical reflection

**Read this paragraph to the group:**

The book of Ephesians is essentially a meditation on the Christian life. Thematically, the book concentrates on Christian unity and the victory of the Holy Spirit over hate and disagreement. This passage deals with the role of speech in Christian unity.

**Have someone read this passage aloud:**

Ephesians 4:15-16:
[15]But speaking the truth in love, we must grow up in every way into him who is the head, into Christ, [16]from whom the whole body, joined and knit together by every ligament with which it is equipped, as each part is working properly, promotes the body's growth in building itself up in love.

**Invite group members to respond to the questions printed below. If time is limited, choose the questions that best meet your group's needs:**

1. What do you think it means to "speak the truth in love"?

2. How does communication affect group unity?

3. In what areas do we need to improve our communication with one another and with others in our congregation?

4. What steps can our group take to improve our communication with one another and with others in our congregation?

## Closing prayer

**Post the following prayer on a chalkboard or newsprint. Then pray as a group:**

*Loving God, we commit ourselves to work at speaking the truth in love. Amen*

## Community Builder 33
# Encouraging One Another

## Opening prayer

**Instruct the group that each time the leader says, "Compassionate God," the group will respond, "Encourage us!"**

Leader:      When we are weak, compassionate God,

Group:      Encourage us!

Leader:      When we are fainthearted, compassionate God,

Group:      Encourage us!

Leader:      When we are idle, compassionate God,

Group:      Encourage us!

## Gathering time

**Ask each person in the group to respond to one of the following:**

■ Describe a courageous act you have done or witnessed.

■ Share a memory of being cheered on as a child.

■ What is some helpful advice you have received?

## Biblical reflection

**Read this paragraph to the group:**

Paul, working with Timothy and Silas, founded the church in Thessalonica. The Thessalonians expected Christ to return at any moment, and some even tried to predict the exact date. Paul encouraged the Thessalonians to concentrate instead on their daily Christian life.

**Have someone read this passage aloud:**

1 Thessalonians 5:11-14:
[11]Therefore encourage one another and build up each other, as indeed you are doing. [12]But we appeal to you, brothers and sisters, to respect those who labor among you, and have charge of you in the Lord and admonish you; [13]esteem them very highly in love because of their work. Be at peace among yourselves. [14]And we urge you, beloved, to admonish the idlers, encourage the faint hearted, help the weak, be patient with all of them.

**Invite group members to respond to the questions printed below. If time is limited, choose the questions that best meet your group's needs:**

1. If you thought the world was ending soon, how would that affect how you lived your life and interacted with others?

2. Recall times when words of encouragement or praise have helped you or our group.

3. In what areas of our group's work do we need encouragement and support?

4. In what ways can our group encourage and support one another as we continue our work in the future?

## Closing prayer

**Tell group members that you will be offering a prayer in which they will be asked to silently name areas in their lives for which they need encouragement. Begin by praying:**

*God, hear our silent prayers for encouragement . . . (pause).*

**When two or three minutes have passed, pray:**

*God of hope, empower us to do what we have asked. Remind us to encourage one another. Amen*

## Community Builder 34

# Coping with Change

## Opening prayer

**Instruct the group that each time the leader says, "Though the earth shall change," the group will respond, "You, steadfast God, will not."**

Leader:     God, you are our refuge and strength. Though the earth shall change,

Group:      You, steadfast God, will not.

Leader:     We have seen the seasons come and go, from birth to death and all the ages in between, our lives move steadily forward. Though the earth shall change,

Group:      You, steadfast God, will not.

## Gathering time

**Ask each person in the group to respond to one of the following:**

■ Describe one of your favorite hiding places as a child.

■ Tell about a major change you have experienced in your life.

■ Tell about an experience on a mountain or other high place.

## Biblical reflection

**Read this paragraph to the group:**

Some scholars believe that this psalm was written to accompany the new-year celebration. In its entirety, the psalm stands as a great expression of faith in God's power. In this passage, the psalmist reminds the hearers that as God brought order out of chaos at the creation of the world, God continues to order the world.

**Have someone read this passage aloud:**

Psalm 46:1-3:
¹God is our refuge and strength, a very present help in trouble. ²Therefore we will not fear, though the earth should change, though the mountains shake in the heart of the sea; ³though its waters roar and foam, though the mountains tremble with its tumult.

**Invite group members to respond to the questions printed below. If time is limited, choose the questions that best meet your group's needs:**

1. In the midst of life's changes, how has God been your refuge and strength?

2. How do you respond to change?

3. How have the changes our group has experienced affected our work?

4. What can we do to help each other cope with these changes?

5. What new possibilities might result from the changes we are encountering?

## Closing prayer

**Tell group members that you will be offering a prayer in which they will be asked to name some of the changes they have experienced, either in their own lives or as a group. Then, pray the following prayer aloud:**

*Mighty God, through all the changes we have experienced, especially those we name before you silently or aloud . . . (pause). Assure us that in the midst of our sometimes chaotic lives exists your perfect order. Amen*

| Community Builder 35 | # Making an Important Decision |
|---|---|

## Opening prayer

**Instruct the group that each time the leader says, "For your name's sake," the group will respond, "Lead us and guide us."**

Leader: God, our rock and our fortress, for your name's sake,

Group: Lead us and guide us.

Leader: As you have faithfully directed our steps in the past, for your name's sake,

Group: Lead us and guide us.

Leader: As we wrestle with important decisions, for your name's sake,

Group: Lead us and guide us.

## Gathering time

**Ask each person in the group to respond to one of the following:**

■ Tell about an important decision you have made.

■ Describe a home you lived in as a child.

■ Share a skill you have mastered that others might consider to be difficult.

## Biblical reflection

**Read this paragraph to the group:**

The first eight verses of this psalm, an individual lament, record the psalmist's prayer for deliverance from danger. According to Luke's Gospel, Jesus' last words came from this psalm (verse 5a).

**Have someone read this passage aloud:**

Psalm 31:3-5:
[3]You are indeed my rock and my fortress; for your name's sake lead me and guide me, [4]take me out of the net that is hidden for me, for you are my refuge. [5]Into your hand I commit my spirit; you have redeemed me, O LORD, faithful God.

**Invite group members to respond to the questions printed below. If time is limited, choose the questions that best meet your group's needs:**

1. The psalmist prays for God's guidance and protection. What do you seek from God when you are making an important decision?

2. What steps has our group found helpful in making important decisions in the past?

3. As you consider the decision we are currently making, what about the process do you find difficult?

4. As we make this current decision, what are your hopes? What are your fears?

## Closing prayer

**Ask group members to share their prayer concerns. Remind them that the mention of a concern is a prayer. Conclude by praying aloud:**

*Into your hands, Spirit of power, we commit these prayers. Amen*

## Community Builder 36

# Facing a Crisis

## Opening prayer

**Pray the following prayer aloud:**

Jesus, support of those who trust in you, we thank you for loving us so much that you hold us close and promise never to let us go. Cling to us, Jesus, today and through whatever lies ahead. Amen

## Gathering time

**Ask each person in the group to respond to one of the following:**

■ Tell about one of your phobias.

■ Describe a memory of being comforted as a child.

■ Tell about a time when you were lost.

## Biblical reflection

**Read this paragraph to the group:**

Paul wrote to the Romans while he was in Corinth, before he had visited Rome. This letter is Paul's most clear and comprehensive expression of his theology. This passage forms the conclusion of a section on Christian freedom. Paul reminds his hearers that nothing in the universe can separate them from God's redeeming love.

**Have someone read this passage aloud:**

Romans 8:35, 37-39:
[35]Who will separate us from the love of Christ? Will hardship, or distress, or persecution, or famine, or nakedness, or peril, or sword? . . . [37]No, in all these things we are more than conquerors through him who loved us. [38]For I am convinced that neither death, nor life, nor angels, nor rulers, nor things present, nor things to come, nor powers, [39]nor height, nor depth, nor anything else in all creation, will be able to separate us from the love of God in Christ Jesus our Lord.

**Invite group members to respond to the questions printed below. If time is limited, choose the questions that best meet your group's needs:**

1. Paul writes that nothing can separate a Christian from God's love. Tell about an experience that illustrates this.

2. What troubles you about the crisis our group is facing?

3. How does this crisis divert us from our tasks?

4. How can we help each other to complete our work in the midst of this crisis?

## Closing prayer

**Ask group members to repeat the following sentence prayer, filling in the blank with their own words:**

*Jesus, do not let _____ separate us from you.*

**It might be helpful to post this prayer on a chalkboard or newsprint. Invite everyone to pray, but say that no one is required to speak. Conclude by praying:**

*Jesus, we trust your love, in the midst of the present crisis and through all that is to come. Amen*

## Community Builder 37

# When We Have Lost Our Focus

## Opening prayer

**Pray the following prayer aloud:**

God of all wanderers, like the ancient people of Israel who wandered in the wilderness, we sometimes lose our way. And like those people of old, we call out to you, O God our guide, asking that you direct us toward the goals you have set before us. Amen

## Gathering time

**Ask each person in the group to respond to one of the following:**

■ Share an experience you had while moving from one home to another.

■ Describe an experience with a camera.

■ Tell about a place in which you have enjoyed wandering.

## Biblical reflection

**Read this paragraph to the group:**

Psalm 107, a psalm of both thanksgiving and wisdom, records the gratitude of four groups of redeemed persons: desert wanderers, prisoners, the sick, and sea travelers. This passage focuses on travelers lost in the desert. In verse eight, not printed here, the psalmist calls the travelers to utter a prayer of thanksgiving to God.

**Have someone read this passage aloud:**

Psalm 107:4-7:
⁴Some wandered in desert wastes, finding no way to an inhabited town; ⁵hungry and thirsty, their soul fainted within them. ⁶Then they cried to the Lord in their trouble, and he delivered them from their distress; ⁷he led them by a straight way, until they reached an inhabited town.

**Invite group members to respond to the questions printed below. If time is limited, choose the questions that best meet your group's needs:**

1. How is the experience of losing one's focus similar to the psalmist's experience of wandering in the desert?

2. What are some of the distractions that our group is currently facing?

3. What are some steps that our group can take toward regaining our focus?

4. In the psalm, God led the wanderers to an inhabited town. Where is God leading our group?

## Closing prayer

**Post the following prayer on a chalkboard or newsprint and pray it together:**

*Guiding God, when we wander, lead us in the path that you would have us follow. Remind us that even when we lose sight of you, you never lose sight of us. Amen*

## Community Builder 38

# When Our Work Becomes a Drudgery

## Opening prayer

**Pray the following prayer aloud:**

God of miracles, sometimes we work long hours and fail to see productive results from our labor. We grow tired and bored by the tasks you have called us to take on. Revive our spirits, renew our vision, and restore our desire to serve you. Amen

## Gathering time

**Ask each person in the group to respond to one of the following:**

■ What household chore do you find most tiring and why?

■ Describe the worst job you have ever had. Why was it bad?

■ Tell about a miracle you have experienced or witnessed.

## Biblical reflection

**Read this paragraph to the group:**

The writer of both Luke and Acts, thought to be a physician, dedicated both books to someone named Theophilus (meaning "lover of God"). Luke's Gospel is known for its focus on Jesus' mission of love to those outsiders most easily overlooked. This passage is part of Jesus' call to the first disciples.

**Have someone read this passage aloud:**

Luke 5:4-6:
⁴When [Jesus] had finished speaking, he said to Simon, "Put out into the deep water and let down your nets for a catch." ⁵Simon answered, "Master, we have worked all night long but have caught nothing. Yet if you say so, I will let down the nets." ⁶When they had done this, they caught so many fish that their nets were beginning to break.

**Invite group members to respond to the questions printed below. If time is limited, choose the questions that best meet your group's needs:**

1. In what ways might fishing have become a drudgery for the disciples?

2. If you had been one of the disciples described in Luke 5:4-6, how might you have reacted to Jesus' miracle?

3. What aspects of our group's work do you find tiring or repetitive?

4. What aspects of our group's work do you still find exciting or interesting?

5. Short of a miracle, what might breathe life back into our work together?

## Closing prayer

**Tell group members that you will be offering a prayer in which they will be asked to thank God for aspects of the group's work that they find fulfilling and exciting. Then, pray the following prayer aloud:**

*Thank you, God, for the opportunity to serve you through our work and especially for . . . (pause).*

**Conclude the prayer by saying:**

*Even when our work becomes a drudgery, never let us fail to see the blessings and opportunities you continue to give us. Amen*

## Community Builder 39

# When We Are Overwhelmed

## Opening prayer

**Pray the following prayer aloud:**

Holy and awesome God, when difficulties arise and life overwhelms, remind us that we belong to you. When fears fill our hearts and doubts cloud our minds, remind us that you have promised to walk with us through it all. Amen

## Gathering time

**Ask each person in the group to respond to one of the following:**

■ Tell about a time when you were homesick.

■ Describe a frightening adventure.

■ Tell about how you received your name.

## Biblical reflection

**Read this paragraph to the group:**

This passage was written to comfort the Jewish people who had been exiled from their home in Judah. It was written toward the end of their sixty years in exile, at a time when the exiled Jews were no doubt despairing over ever returning home again. The prophet wrote both to encourage them and to renew their faith in Yahweh as the God who will save them.

**Have someone read this passage aloud:**

Isaiah 43:1-2:
¹But now thus says the LORD, he who created you, O Jacob, he who formed you, O Israel: Do not fear, for I have redeemed you; I have called you by name, you are mine. ²When you pass through the waters, I will be with you; and through the rivers, they shall not overwhelm you; when you walk through the fire you shall not be burned, and the flame shall not consume you.

**Invite group members to respond to the questions printed below. If time is limited, choose the questions that best meet your group's needs:**

1. How would Isaiah's words be a comfort to people overwhelmed by the challenges of living in a foreign land?

2. Isaiah uses the images of walking through water and fire to describe the feeling of being overwhelmed. How would you describe the feeling of being overwhelmed?

3. What tasks, events, or experiences are overwhelming to our group now?

4. What can we do to complete our tasks even though we are feeling overwhelmed?

5. What message does our group need to hear from God right now?

## Closing prayer

**Invite group members to complete the following sentence prayer with the name of the person on their right:**

*Thank you, God, for redeeming (name), and calling him/her by name.*

**It might be helpful to post this prayer on a chalkboard or newsprint. When all have been prayed for, conclude by praying:**

*God of water and fire, through all that we face continue to remind us that we belong to you. Amen*

## Community Builder 40

# When We Have Failed at a Task

## Opening prayer

**Pray the following prayer aloud:**

God of new beginnings, though we start with good intentions and great hopes of success, many times we fail and need to begin again. Lift us up when we fall, shine a light in our darkness, and give us the determination to resume our tasks. Amen

## Gathering time

**Ask each person in the group to respond to one of the following:**

- Tell about a time when you waited for someone with anticipation.
- Describe an experience of losing a game.
- Tell about a time when you fell.

## Biblical reflection

**Read this paragraph to the group:**

In the time that Micah wrote, the Jewish people were divided into two kingdoms—the Northern Kingdom (also called Israel) and the Southern Kingdom (also referred to as Judah). Micah came from the town of Moresheth, a village west of Jerusalem in the Southern Kingdom. He prophesied against Israel's sins and predicted the fall of the Northern Kingdom. In this passage, Micah pledges his trust in God and God's promise of salvation.

**Have someone read this passage aloud:**

Micah 7:7-8:

⁷But as for me, I will look to the LORD, I will wait for the God of my salvation; my God will hear me. ⁸Do not rejoice over me, O my enemy; when I fall, I shall rise; when I sit in darkness, the LORD will be a light to me.

**Invite group members to respond to the questions printed below. If time is limited, choose the questions that best meet your group's needs:**

1. Micah expresses that, from God's perspective, times of failure and difficulty are temporary. Share experiences of yours that illustrate this.

2. What have you found most difficult about the experience of failing at a task?

3. What have we learned from this experience that will help our group in our future work?

4. How might God make good things come out of this difficult experience?

## Closing prayer

**Tell group members that you will be offering a prayer in which they will be asked to thank God for the successes that your group has experienced in its work together. Begin by praying:**

*Saving God, we thank you for the successes by which you have blessed our work together . . . (pause).*

**Conclude by praying:**

*You are the God of our salvation. When we fall, you will raise us up. Amen*

## Community Builder 41

# When We Feel Discouraged

## Opening prayer

**Pray the following prayer aloud:**

God who walks with us, sustain us with your presence when we cannot hear your voice. Embrace us with your love when we do not feel you near us. Hold our discouraged souls in your hands and revive in us the ability to dream. Amen

## Gathering time

**Ask each person in the group to respond to one of the following:**

■ Describe a time when you laughed uncontrollably.

■ Share one of your favorite ways of cheering yourself up when you are discouraged.

■ Tell about a time you stayed up all night.

## Biblical reflection

**Read this paragraph to the group:**

In this psalm of lament, the writer describes the experience of feeling abandoned by God. Yet, in the midst of this forsakenness, the psalmist still claims faith in God when referring to God as "My God." In the middle of the psalm, the mood changes and the psalmist rejoices in God's deliverance. Jesus spoke the words, "My God, my God, why have you forsaken me?" as he was dying on the cross.

**Have someone read this passage aloud:**

Psalm 22:1-2:
¹My God, my God, why have you forsaken me? Why are you so far from helping me, from the words of my groaning? ²O my God, I cry by day, but you do not answer; and by night, but find no rest.

**Invite group members to respond to the questions printed below. If time is limited, choose the questions that best meet your group's needs:**

1. The psalmist felt abandoned by God. What is the experience of feeling discouraged like for you?

2. The psalmist said, "My God, my God, why have you forsaken me?" What do you want to say to God right now?

3. In the midst of feeling discouraged, what are some of the encouraging aspects of our group's work together?

4. The psalmist experienced a change of mood and rejoiced in God's deliverance. What would it take for our group to move from discouragement into rejoicing?

## Closing prayer

**Ask each group member to pray for the person on his or her right, saying these words:**

*Ever-present God, do not let (name) be discouraged.*

**When everyone has been prayed for, conclude by praying:**

*God, our rock and salvation, give our group the courage we need to continue our work of serving you. Amen*

## Community Builder 42

# Persisting in the Midst of Difficulty

## Opening prayer

**Pray the following prayer aloud:**

Jesus, fountain of life, sometimes our burdens grow heavy and we feel unable to continue in our task of serving you. Refresh our spirits and restore our courage to persist, so that in the face of difficulty we may press forward with hope. Amen

## Gathering time

**Ask each person in the group to respond to one of the following:**

■ Tell a story about a surprise visitor.

■ Describe an experience of searching for a lost valuable.

■ Share an experience from your life that illustrates the saying, "If at first you don't succeed, try, try again."

## Biblical reflection

**Read this paragraph to the group:**

This passage, from Jesus' sermon on the mount, is about the power of prayer. Jesus assures his followers that God hears their petitions and encourages them to bring all of their concerns to God.

**Have someone read this passage aloud:**

Matthew 7:7-8:
[Jesus said,] [7]"Ask, and it will be given you; search, and you will find; knock, and the door will be opened for you. [8]For everyone who asks receives, and everyone who searches finds, and for everyone who knocks, the door will be opened."

**Invite group members to respond to the questions printed below. If time is limited, choose the questions that best meet your group's needs:**

1. What do you find surprising about Jesus' words in Matthew 7:7-8?

2. What do you think Jesus meant when he said, "Ask and it will be given you"?

3. How would you translate Jesus' words about persisting into a specific message for our group?

4. What doors would you like God to open for our group?

## Closing prayer

**Share the following sentence prayer with group members and ask them to complete it with their own prayer concerns:**

*Giver of life, we ask for _____.*

**It might be helpful to post this prayer on a chalkboard or newsprint. When you have provided adequate time for all who wish to participate, conclude by praying:**

*Giver of life, we ask, we search, we knock on the door. Hear our prayer. Amen*

## Community Builder 43

# When We Have Disagreements

## Opening prayer

**Pray the following prayer aloud:**

God of peace, we thank you for the gift of each other. Though we all desire to serve you, we confess that sometimes we disagree with one another. Show us how we can overcome our differences and unite in our work for you. Amen

## Gathering time

**Ask each person in the group to respond to one of the following:**

■ Tell about a childhood quarrel you had with a sibling or a friend.

■ Tell about a time that your family did something together that you especially enjoyed.

■ Share something you appreciate about being a part of this group.

## Biblical reflection

**Read this paragraph to the group:**

Paul's letter to the Corinthian church deals with such pastoral concerns as congregational divisions, immorality, and disputes over theological doctrine. The members of the Corinthian church formed factions around teachers and apostles and then fought about who preached the true Christ.

**Have someone read this passage aloud:**

1 Corinthians 1:10-13:

[10]Now I appeal to you, brothers and sisters, by the name of our Lord Jesus Christ, that all of you be in agreement and that there be no divisions among you, but that you be united in the same mind and the same purpose. [11]For it has been reported to me by Chloe's people that there are quarrels among you, my brothers and sisters. [12]What I mean is that each of you says, "I belong to Paul," or "I belong to Apollos," or " belong to Cephas," or "I belong to Christ." [13]Has Christ been divided? Was Paul crucified for you? Or were you baptized in the name of Paul?

**Invite group members to respond to the questions printed below. If time is limited, choose the questions that best meet your group's needs:**

1. What advice would you have given to the congregation at Corinth to help them resolve their differences?

2. In what ways might your advice to the Christians at Corinth be helpful in our own situation?

3. What unites us as a group?

4. What can we do to help our group keep focused on our tasks when we have disagreements?

## Closing prayer

**Begin by praying:**

*We thank you, creator Spirit, for the blessings we share, including those we name before you both silently and aloud . . . (pause).*

**Conclude by praying aloud:**

*Help us to work through our disagreements and concentrate on serving you. Amen*

## Community Builder 44

# Respecting One Another in the Midst of Conflict

## Opening prayer

**Pray the following prayer aloud:**

Faithful and just God, give us the vision and the courage to respect one another even in the midst of conflict. Set before us Jesus' example of humility and remind us of his command to love one another. Amen

## Gathering time

**Ask each person in the group to respond to one of the following:**

■ Tell about an unselfish act you have done or witnessed.

■ Describe someone you respect although his or her opinions or values differ from your own.

■ Tell about a "fight" you had with a major household appliance.

## Biblical reflection

**Read this paragraph to the group:**

Paul wrote this letter to the Philippians to thank them. In this passage, Paul counsels the Philippians to let humility guide their actions toward one another. He sets Jesus before them as the perfect example of humility, quoting—in the verses that immediately follow this passage—an early belief-statement about Christ.

**Have someone read this passage aloud:**

Philippians 2:3-5:
³Do nothing from selfish ambition or conceit, but in humility regard others as better than yourselves. ⁴Let each of you look not to your own interests, but to the interests of others. ⁵Let the same mind be in you that was in Christ Jesus.

**Invite group members to respond to the questions printed below. If time is limited, choose the questions that best meet your group's needs:**

1. What do you think it means to "regard others as better than yourselves"? (See Philippians 2:3).

2. How might following Paul's advice in Philippians 2:3-5 help people who are engaged in conflict?

3. What might make it difficult for people to respect one another in the midst of conflict?

4. What are some of the qualities that you respect about each other? (Be sure that the qualities of each person in the group are mentioned).

5. What can we do as a group to both "regard others as better than" ourselves and look "to the interests of others"?

## Closing prayer

**Post the following sentence prayer on chalkboard or newsprint:**

*Loving God, may our group be a community where _____'s (name) gifts are appreciated and her/his faith is nurtured.*

**Invite group members to pray this prayer in unison for each member of your group.**

## Community Builder 45

# Forgiving One Another

## Opening prayer

**Pray the following prayer aloud:**

Jesus, our Savior, when we lose sight of you and become focused on ourselves, forgive us. When we allow our differences to divide us, forgive us. When we neglect to attend to the tasks that you have called us to do, forgive us. Amen

## Gathering time

**Ask each person in the group to respond to one of the following:**

■ Tell about a time when, as a child, you needed to say you were sorry.

■ Tell what you do to relieve stress.

■ Share a story about forgiveness that you find inspiring.

## Biblical reflection

**Read this paragraph to the group:**

In chapter 18 of Matthew's Gospel, Jesus taught about how to live in Christian community. Jesus instructed his followers about what to do when a church member sins. In this passage, Jesus' admonition to forgive "seventy-seven times" suggests that one's forgiveness of another needs to be unlimited.

Matthew 18:21-22:
²¹Then Peter came and said to [Jesus], "Lord, if another member of the church sins against me, how often should I forgive? As many as seven times?" ²² Jesus said to him, "Not seven times, but, I tell you, seventy-seven times."

**Invite group members to respond to the questions printed below. If time is limited, choose the questions that best meet your group's needs:**

1. What makes it difficult for people to forgive one another?

2. What are some of the limits and conditions people put on forgiveness? Are some of these appropriate?

3. In what ways are forgiveness and tolerance or acceptance distinct from one another? How are they related?

4. Why is forgiveness important for a group to function well?

5. How can we make forgiveness an ongoing reality for our group?

## Closing prayer

**Tell group members that during the following prayer, you will provide time for silent confession:**

Leader:     Jesus, we silently confess that we have sinned against you and one another. (Allow time for private prayer.)

Leader:     Jesus our Savior has promised to forgive us and asks all who follow him to forgive one another. May God grant us the grace to do this. Amen

## Community Builder 46

# Finding Solutions to Problems

## Opening prayer

**Pray the following prayer aloud:**

Faithful God, in the midst of problems and difficulties, we may feel confused and alone. Remind us of your presence and your promise to guide us to new solutions. Amen

## Gathering time

**Ask each person in the group to respond to one of the following:**

■ Describe an experience taking a test.

■ Tell about a time when you used your ingenuity to solve a problem.

■ If you wrote an etiquette column, what would your number one piece of advice be and why?

## Biblical reflection

**Read this paragraph to the group:**

Just prior to this passage, Paul used the Israelites' rebellious behavior in the wilderness as a warning to the Christians in Corinth. The Corinthian Christians were known to Paul for their sometimes corrupt behavior. In this verse, Paul reminds the Corinthians that even in the midst of testing, God is faithful.

**Have someone read this passage aloud:**

1 Corinthians 10:13:
[13]No testing has overtaken you that is not common to everyone. God is faithful, and he will not let you be tested beyond your strength, but with the testing he will also provide the way out so that you may be able to endure it.

**Invite group members to respond to the questions printed below. If time is limited, choose the questions that best meet your group's needs:**

1. First Corinthians 10:13 suggests that God provides solutions to problems. Share experiences from your life that illustrate this.

2. How has God helped our group or other groups to solve problems in the past?

3. What can we learn from those past experiences that we can apply to solving our current problems?

4. How does hearing that "God will not let you be tested beyond your strength" comfort and motivate you as we seek to find solutions to our problems?

## Closing prayer

**Tell group members that you will be offering a prayer in which they will be asked to silently thank God for leading them through difficult situations in the past. Begin by praying:**

*Guiding God, we thank you for providing us with strength to endure the tests and trials of our lives . . . (pause).*

**When two or three minutes have passed, conclude by praying:**

*Guiding God, continue to strengthen us as we cope with the problems we now face. Amen*

## Community Builder 47

# Saying Thanks

## Opening prayer

**Instruct the group that each time the leader says, "We thank you," the group will respond, "We praise you, O God."**

Leader:     For renewing our energy when we grow weary of our tasks, we thank you;

Group:      We praise you, O God.

Leader:     For prodding us forward when we become stuck in our ways, we thank you;

Group:      We praise you, O God.

Leader:     For opening our eyes to new possibilities when we cannot see the way, we thank you;

Group:      We praise you, O God.

## Gathering time

**Ask each person in the group to respond to one of the following:**

■ Tell about a unique way you once demonstrated your thankfulness to someone.

■ Tell about a surprising or meaningful thank-you note you received.

■ Who in your life, past or present, would you most like to thank and why?

## Biblical reflection

**Read this paragraph to the group:**

Paul wrote to the Thessalonians shortly after Timothy had returned from Thessalonica with a positive report about that church. In much of First Thessalonians, Paul shares his feelings of thanksgiving and love for them. This passage is part of Paul's concluding exhortations and greetings.

**Have someone read this passage aloud:**

1 Thessalonians 5:16-18:
[16]Rejoice always, [17]pray without ceasing, [18]give thanks in all circumstances; for this is the will of God in Christ Jesus for you.

**Invite group members to respond to the questions printed below. If time is limited, choose the questions that best meet your group's needs:**

1. When do you find it difficult to follow Paul's advice to give thanks in all circumstances?

2. Who does our group need to thank and how might we do that?

3. When you consider our work together, for what are you most thankful to God?

4. How does saying thanks in all circumstances affect one's life?

5. How might saying thanks affect our group as we approach our tasks?

## Closing prayer

**Tell group members that you will be concluding with a sentence prayer. They may complete the sentence as often as they like:**

*Ever-living God, we thank you for _____.*

## Community Builder 48

# Celebrating Accomplishments

## Opening prayer

**Pray the following prayer aloud:**

God, provider for the universe, everything that our group has accomplished has come as a gift from you. Show us your hand at work in all that we do. Celebrate with us now as we rejoice in your blessings. Amen

## Gathering time

**Ask each person in the group to respond to one of the following:**

■ If you had unlimited resources to celebrate a personal accomplishment, what would you do?

■ Whose accomplishments do you most admire and why?

■ Describe a memorable celebration you attended.

## Biblical reflection

**Read this paragraph to the group:**

First and Second Chronicles, originally one book, recount Israel's history from the time of Adam to the end of the Babylonian exile. Much of 1 Chronicles is devoted to the story of King David's rule over Israel. This passage is part of David's speech in which he urges his hearers to provide financial support for the building and maintenance of the temple.

**Have someone read this passage aloud:**

1 Chronicles 29:10, 13-14:
<sup>10</sup>Then David blessed the LORD in the presence of all the assembly; David said: "Blessed are you, O LORD, the God of our ancestor Israel, forever and ever. . . . <sup>13</sup>And now, our God, we give thanks to you and praise your glorious name. <sup>14</sup>But who am I, and what is my people, that we should be able to make this freewill offering? For all things come from you, and of your own have we given you."

**Invite group members to respond to the questions printed below. If time is limited, choose the questions that best meet your group's needs:**

1. David gave thanks to God for accomplishing the important task of raising money for the temple. How might celebrating accomplishments motivate and inspire our group?

2. Where do you see God at work in the accomplishments of our group?

3. What do you find most gratifying about the tasks our group has accomplished?

4. What are some ways we can acknowledge and celebrate our group's accomplishments?

## Closing prayer

**Tell group members that you will be offering a prayer in which they will be asked to name some of their group's accomplishments. Begin by praying:**

*God, giver of all good things, we thank you for all that you have inspired us to accomplish, including those tasks we name before you now . . . (pause).*

**Conclude by praying:**

*Merciful God, all things come from you, and of your own we have given you. Amen*

## Community Builder 49

# At the End of a Year

## Opening prayer

**Pray the following prayer aloud:**

Eternal God, as we look back on the year that has been and ahead to the year to come, we thank you for your constant, unchanging presence through all the seasons of our lives. Continue to inspire our group in the future as you have in the past. Direct the work we do in your name. Amen

## Gathering time

**Ask each person in the group to respond to one of the following:**

■ What is your favorite season and why?

■ Tell about a birth you witnessed.

■ Tell about a personal or family New Year's tradition.

## Biblical reflection

**Read this paragraph to the group:**

Ecclesiastes, meaning "teacher," was written by a professional sage. The book is classified as wisdom literature because the writer sought to find meaning in the midst of life's seeming futility. These verses are an excerpt from one of the most well-known passages in Ecclesiastes—the writer's meditation on time.

**Have someone read this passage aloud:**

Ecclesiastes 3:1-2:
[1]For everything there is a season, and a time for every matter under heaven: [2]a time to be born, and a time to die; a time to plant, and a time to pluck up what is planted.

**Invite group members to respond to the questions printed below. If time is limited, choose the questions that best meet your group's needs:**

1. As you look back on the past year, which of our group's accomplishments are you most proud of and why?

2. If we could relive this year, what would you do differently?

3. What opportunities and challenges await our group in the coming year?

4. What does our group most need to hear from God at the end of this year together?

5. The writer of Ecclesiastes says that there is a time for everything. What is it time for in our group?

## Closing prayer

**Tell group members that you will be offering a prayer in which they will be invited to name their hopes for the future of your group. Begin by praying:**

*God of all times and seasons, we name before you, both silently and aloud, our hopes and dreams for the future of this group . . . (pause).*

**When all have finished, pray aloud:**

*Into your hands, redeemer God, we commend our hopes and dreams. Guide us into the future. Amen*

## Community Builder 50

# For the End of a Group

## Opening prayer

**Pray the following prayer aloud:**

We thank you, God of our hopes, for the life you have given to our group. We thank you for the tasks we have accomplished in your name and for bringing us closer both to you and to one another. We thank you for leading us through difficult moments and celebrating with us the joyous ones. We thank you, God of our hopes. Amen

## Gathering time

**Ask each person in the group to respond to one of the following:**

■ Tell about a time when it was difficult for you to say good-bye.

■ Tell about an ending that you welcomed or were glad to experience.

■ If you could write an epitaph for this group, what would it be and why?

## Biblical reflection

**Read this paragraph to the group:**

Paul wrote this thank-you letter to the congregation at Philippi from prison. The Philippians were the only congregation from whom Paul accepted financial support. In this passage, Paul expresses his thanks and promises to pray for the congregation at Philippi.

**Have someone read this passage aloud:**

Philippians 1:3-6:

[3]I thank my God every time I remember you, [4]constantly praying with joy in every one of my prayers for all of you, [5]because of your sharing in the gospel from the first day until now. [6]I am confident of this, that the one who began a good work among you will bring it to completion by the day of Jesus Christ.

**Invite group members to respond to the questions printed below. If time is limited, choose the questions that best meet your group's needs:**

1. Paul wrote, "I thank my God every time I remember you." Who and what do you thank God for when you remember the time you spent in this group?

2. How has God brought to completion the work we have done together?

3. How has our group's work affected the life of our congregation or community?

4. In what ways will our work continue to influence or affect the congregation?

5. How do each of you plan to serve God in the future?

## Closing prayer

**Ask group members to pray for the person on their right using the following prayer:**

*God of our hopes, bless (name), in all that he/she does to serve you in the future.*

**It might be helpful to post this prayer on a chalkboard or newsprint.**